THE LORE AND
LEGENDS
OF WALL STREET

THE LORE AND LEGENDS OF WALL STREET

Robert M. Sharp

Dow Jones-Irwin
Homewood, Illinois 60430

© RICHARD D. IRWIN, INC., 1989

Dow Jones-Irwin is a trademark of Dow Jones & Company, Inc.

This publication is designed to provide accurate and
authoritative information in regard to the subject matter
covered. It is sold with the understanding that the
publisher is not engaged in rendering legal, accounting, or
other professional service. If legal advice or other expert
assistance is required, the services of a competent
professional person should be sought.

*From a Declaration of Principles jointly adopted by a Committee
of the American Bar Association and a Committee of Publishers.*

Project editor: Waivah Clement
Production manager: Ann Cassady
Jacket designer: Tim Kaage
Sketches by Sarah S. Sharp
Compositor: TCSystems, Inc.
Typeface: 11/13 Times Roman
Printer: R. R. Donnelley & Sons Company

Library of Congress Cataloging-in-Publication Data

Sharp, Robert M.
  The lore and legends of Wall Street.

  Bibliography: p.
  1. Wall Street—History. I. Title.
HG4572.S43 1989   332.64'273   88–33536
ISBN 1-55623-151-2

Printed in the United States of America

1 2 3 4 5 6 7 8 9 0 DO 6 5 4 3 2 1 0 9

PREFACE

Three centuries ago my immigrant ancestor, John Sharp, sold a piece of land in New Jersey and moved to Manhattan. This insignificant scrap of information is one of thousands discovered while researching my family line. I had traced the Sharps back to Perth Amboy, New Jersey, where 10 generations earlier, John Sharp had sought a better life as an indentured servant in America after leaving Scotland in "the killing time."

While methodically compiling family history, I was also working on a retirement generously provided by the stock market and giving seminars on stock market strategy. To keep these seminars interesting (for me if not for the students), I was reading financial history for anecdotes to liven the presentation.

Soon I was hooked on both projects, corresponding with the New-York Historical Society, digging through 17th-century tax rolls and Common Council notes, and reconstructing old maps.

Then the two projects merged! I found that I was reading about John Sharp, Frederick Philipse, and William Kidd on the same page. In 1696, John Sharp bought a lot, built a house, was given the freedom of the city (licensed) as a carpenter, and went to work on Trinity Church. His house was just off Wall on William, catercorner from Captain William Kidd's home on the north side of Wall. In the business district on Pearl Street, Frederick Philipse was Manhattan's first tycoon.

John Sharp's property tax for 1697 was a fathom of white wampum to be used in support of the poor. The city had some 3,000 citizens and 900 taxpayers. John must have tired of high taxes and congested city life, for he moved back to Perth Amboy after the completion of Trinity Church. Soon after, the wall was torn down and the street began to develop.

This is the story of that street—Wall Street—the events that shaped it, and the characters that made and lost fortunes in the arenas that flanked it. This text is not meant to be a definitive history and is not restricted to Wall Street when there is a story about speculation worth telling. If you desire more detail, the bibliography should be useful. Each story was a delightful discovery for me and I hope you enjoy them too!

ACKNOWLEDGMENTS

My first book, *Calculated Risk,* came from my own experience, but this book required a lot of help. Particularly cooperative were the librarians and public relations officers of the stock exchanges around the world. The New York, American, London, and Amsterdam exchanges all responded to requests for information and historical matter. Mr. J. Sas of the Amsterdam Bourse sent me a replica of the oldest certificate, a number of historical pieces and pictures. He also answered my questions about use of the Dutch language.

Ms. Mariam Touba of the New-York Historical Society researched Leonard Bleecker and Frederick Philipse for me, actually typing one old document that was beyond electronic copying. Ms. Evelyn L. Klingler of the Morris County (New Jersey) Free Library supplied a number of documents on the Morris Canal. Chase Manhattan Bank and Merrill Lynch provided histories of their companies, and Brown Brothers supplied the old photographs.

Special thanks goes to Haley Garrison (Antique Stocks and Bonds) of Williamsburg, Virginia, who encouraged the work and suggested some of the stories. Laurie Brannen of Plaza Communications started the process by publishing "Legends and Lore" in *Personal Investor* and *Registered Representative* magazines.

Last but not least, this was a family affair. My daughter, Sarah Suzanne Sharp, did the sketches and took the photo used on the flap. My son David did the word processing and my wife, Esther Mary, proofed the manuscript. My son Daniel and his bride, Betsy, provided incentive, as the royalty advance was used to purchase a wedding present of one share of Berkshire Hathaway.

Robert M. Sharp

CONTENTS

PART 3   THE GILDED AGE (1848–1872)

PART 4   THE MONEY GAME (1875–1901)

PART 5   THE GLOBAL STREET (1907–1939)

PART 6 THE COMPUTER AGE (1949–   )

INTRODUCTION

The business of trading goods began with man's origins and speculation quickly followed. Food could be traded for simple tools or weapons in expectation of producing even more food. Needs soon became more sophisticated, and trading with remote parts of the world became desirable. Great networks were formed by the Phoenician, Greek, Roman, and Byzantine empires, with trade conducted on a barter or cash and carry basis.

The decline of the Roman empire in Europe resulted in disorganized feudal states and isolated European markets from the Asian trade depots. It was not until the 12th century that trade in western Europe began to flourish again.

By 1114, two great trading centers were operating in northern Italy and in Flanders (now Holland and Belgium). The Italians had connections to the far east, and Flanders traded with England and Scandinavia. The counts of Champagne held land on the trade routes and operated trade fairs for international exchange. They provided protection, money changers, and storage facilities for a fee. There were six six-week fairs each year.

These fairs originated the use of brokers—the middlemen of exchange—to introduce buyer and seller. The term *broker* comes from the French *brochier*, which describes one that broached or tapped a wine keg. The term was first applied to the enterpreneurs that bought wine by the barrel from farmers and then sold it by the cup from an appended tap.

Because of the varied ethnic and geographical backgrounds of the traders, a code of commercial law—called the law merchant—soon developed. This defined contract terms and specified the date and place for delivery of goods. This forward (future) contract, called a *lettre de faire,* quickly became an instrument for trade that would change hands a number of times before delivery of the goods.

Soon speculators were assuming the price risk of the merchants by buying the futures contracts and trading these instruments among themselves. This added to the liquidity of trading and contributed to stability for the markets.

From periodic fairs, trading progressed to continuous markets, and the city of Bruges was a prominent early site. A patrician family living there by the name of van den Burse had their name added to the investment lexicon. Their family coat of arms had three moneybags, or purses (*bursa*), and was displayed on their house. This house, called De Burse, was used by Venetian merchants to conduct trade. The name progressed to Beurs and then to Bourse, which became the name applied to European exchanges.

The first building constructed explicitly for commodities exchange was in Antwerp in 1531. Its architecture and open courtyard became a model for future 16th- and 17th-century bourses. Exchanges were founded in Lyons in 1546, Cologne in 1553, and London in 1566. Paris didn't have a legal bourse until 1724.

Merchants actively sought outlets for their wares, and 16th-century exploration was motivated and financed mostly by this need. Trade with the Orient—China and Japan—was particularly desirable, and shorter routes were continually sought. Markets moved from overland trade routes to the docks, where trade flourished in spices, cloth, metals, and foods.

The fairs of Flanders gave way to the bourses of Bruges and Antwerp, which in turn were replaced by the docks of Amsterdam, London, and New York. Joint-stock companies were introduced in 1553, and the first exchange devoted to stocks appeared in Amsterdam in 1602.

Markets in the United States followed this same progression, with commodities traded on the East River docks of Manhattan. Securities were introduced during and after the Revolutionary War, traded in auctions with other commodities, until the need for and interest in a separate market was created.

After the initial interest in the finances of the young nation subsided, the U.S. securities markets languished until railroads and war between the states stimulated industry. Trading then spilled over from the New York Stock and Exchange Board into the many street markets that were born to satisfy America's need for speculation.

Robber barons soon appeared on the Street to manipulate companies and their share prices. Gigantic struggles for domination carried into the early 20th century when regulation and supervision made markets more systematic and fair.

Today computers and communications have created a global marketplace with physical trading arenas virtually unneeded. A telephone and established credit will let you trade commodities or securities anywhere in the world in a matter of minutes. The human element is fast disappearing, and market activity will soon be a faint image of its more colorful past.

PART 1

THE COLONIAL PERIOD
(1553–1720)

CHAPTER 1

THE MERCHANT ADVENTURERS (1553)

In May 1553, three ships commanded by Sir Hugh Willoughby set sail from London seeking a northeast route to China. The expedition progressed down the Thames, past the Greenwich site where 15-year-old King Edward VI of England lay dying, and steered for the Norwegian coast.

In case they were separated, the ships planned to rendezvous at Vardo on the North Cape. This was the point of farthest exploration by western Europeans, and the great "unknowen" lay beyond. Vardo is a fishing village on the extreme northeast coast of Norway, not far from Finland and Russia.

Two months after departure, the ships were separated by a storm. One boat, captained by Richard Chancellor, made Vardo, but the other two—still in contact with each other—overshot Vardo and decided to press on with the exploration while summer lasted. The vessels reached the desolate coast of Novaya Zemlya, but a leaky ship and poor weather forced them to return to the safe harbor of Russian Lapland for the winter. Their intention was to wait for the thaw, resuming the journey in the spring. However, these adventurers had seen their last spring; Russian fishermen found the boats in 1554 with all hands dead of scurvy.

Meanwhile, the third ship had resumed the voyage and, following the coast east of Vardo, found the White Sea. Charged with finding passage to Cathay, the ship sailed to the south end, where the adventurers encountered fishermen and discovered they were in the territory of the Czar of Muscovy. Russia was then known to western Europe only by vague report.

Leaving their ship at Archangel for the winter, the Englishmen accompanied local tribesmen 700 miles overland to Moscow and the court of Ivan the Terrible. Ivan was glad to open a new trade route with the West, and Chancellor returned to Moscow in 1555 with goods to trade. It was then that he learned of Willoughby's fate and was given the logs and other papers from the two ill-fated vessels.

The three ships in this adventure belonged to the first joint-stock company, a novel scheme by London merchants to finance the search for new markets. Before this, the merchants had funded exploration among themselves, to the extent of their resources. In 1551, Sebastian Cabot proposed a company that would be offered to the public in 25-pound shares. The initial subscription was for 6,000 pounds, and Cabot was appointed governor of "the Mysterie and Companie of Merchant Adventurers for the Discovery of Regions, Dominions, Islands and places Unknowen." After relations were established with the Russians, it was popularly known as the Muscovy Company.

Sebastian Cabot had accompanied his father, John, on his voyage to North America in 1498, exploring as far south as Maryland. Sebastian's own career as an explorer wasn't well-documented, but he developed a reputation as an expert in navigation and geography. This led to the position as pilot-major of Spain, and it was only after his return to England in 1548 that the Muscovy Company was conceived.

The genius of the joint-stock company was the formal separation and ownership of shares, allowing the free exchange of equity without the consent of others.

The Muscovy Company prospered, carrying on a thriving business with Russia, but it still sought the riches of China. Company agents went down the Volga to the Caspian Sea and then picked up Marco Polo's overland route to China. But the politics of China forced the company to settle for trade with Persia until that nation was overrun by Turkey in 1580.

The Muscovy Company was the first publicly owned company, and shares traded in London were the first exchanged. These shares were handled like a commodity in private transaction between individuals.

The joint-stock company now became the model for exploration efforts of other nations, and public interest in stocks was almost immediate. Shares, in all cases, were first traded on commodities exchanges until increased demand and the specialized interest dictated the need for a separate exchange. The first of these appeared in Holland nearly 50 years later.

CHAPTER 2

BLUE CHIPS IN A GOLDEN AGE (1602)

On March 20, 1602, the States General of the Netherlands chartered the United East India Company, granting it a monopoly on trade east of the Cape of Good Hope. The charter authorized an initial capital of 6.6 million guilders to be raised by public subscription.

The company had been formed from six private shipping concerns vying for the trade to India, raising capital on a voyage-by-voyage basis. The profits—if any—were distributed on completion of each expedition.

The initial offering was closed on August 31, 1602, with a payment schedule to be completed by September 1606. At that time, a certificate was to be issued. To transfer shares, the buyer had to accompany the seller to the company offices to record and verify the transaction.

Thus did Holland's Golden Age begin—a century of general affluence in commerce, politics, and art and a period when virtually all financial products and trading mechanics developed.

The United East India Company was to become the first blue-chip stock. In 1602, the first market devoted to stocks was established on an Amsterdam bridge over the Amstel River, actively trading the shares of stock held by thousands of Dutch investors.

Only a few days after the original subscription, the shares were so actively traded that they were 15 percent above par, and by 1607 the price had doubled. Speculation was rampant because of poor communications with company operations in distant lands. Out of this speculation sprang a variety of products used today in

FIGURE 2–1
United East India Company Certificate (1606) (*front*)

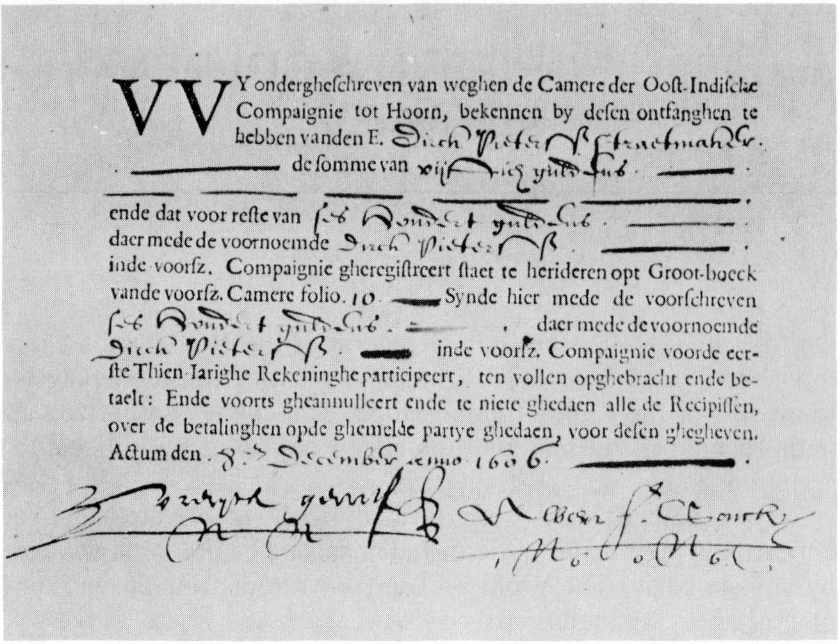

VVY onderghefchreven van weghen de Camere der Ooft-Indifche Compaignie tot Hoorn, bekennen by defen ontfanghen te hebben vanden E. Dirck Pietersz Straetmaker. de fomme van vijftich gulden.
ende dat voor refte van ses hondert gulden. daer mede de voornoemde Dirck Pietersz. inde voorfz. Compaignie gheregiftreert ftaet te herideren opt Groot-boeck vande voorfz. Camere folio. 10 Synde hier mede de voorfchreven ses hondert gulden. daer mede de voornoemde Dirck Pietersz. inde voorfz. Compaignie voorde eerfte Thien-Iarighe Rekeninghe participeert, ten vollen opghebracht ende betaelt: Ende voorts gheannulleert ende te niete ghedaen alle de Recipiffen, over de betalinghen opde ghemelde partye ghedaen, voor defen ghegheven. Actum den 8en December anno 1606.

Courtesy of Amsterdam Stock Exchange

The translation of the front side is as follows:

We the undersigned on behalf of the "Camere der Oost-Indische Compaignie" at Hoom, acknowledge to have received from (Mr. Dirck Pietersz, Straetmaker) the amount of (fifty guilders) being the remainder of (six hundred guilders) for which amount forementioned (Dirck Pietersz.) has been registered by the "Compaignie" to inherit from the Great Book of the "Camere" folio (10.) Being brought in and paid in full the amount of (six hundred guilders) for which the said (Dirck Pietersz.) participates in the first Ten Years Account of the "Compaignie." Being cancelled and annulled all receipts on payments made for the goods mentioned. Actum (December 8, 1606.)

FIGURE 2–2
United East India Company Certificate (1606) (*reverse*)

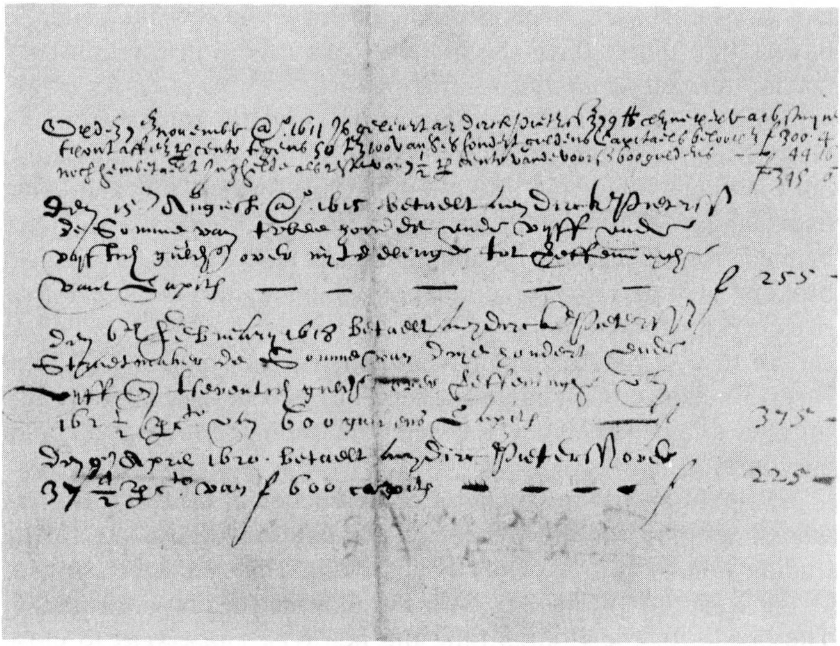

Courtesy of Amsterdam Stock Exchange

On the reverse side is a handwritten list of payments made to the owner of the "actie". A translation follows:

On November 7, anno 1611 were delivered to Dirck Pietersz 379 pounds of
pepper of 16 pennies a pound or in percents 50 per hundred of the amount of   fl. 300, 4, 0
six hundred guilders
and paid in cash as interest of 7½ percent of 600 guilders

fl. 44,16, 0
_____
fl. 345, 0, 0

On August 15, anno 1615 paid to Dirck Pietersz. the amount of two hundred
and fifty-five guilders as repayment for amortization   fl. 255,-

On February 6, 1618 paid to Dirck Pietersz. Straetmaker the amount of
three hundred and seventy-five guilders as liquidation of 62½ percent of
600 guilders   fl. 375,-

On April 9, 1620 paid to Dirck Pietersz. re 37½ percent of 600 guilders   fl. 225,-

virtually the same fashion. Isaac Le Marie formed the first "pool" and sold short large blocks of the stock, while spreading unfavorable rumors. Stock-jobbing was conducted on borrowed money, and contracts were sold on products not owned by the seller to buyers that didn't have the money to buy them in a promissory fashion termed *windhandel*—trading air!

Holland's inclement weather would drive the traders from the New Bridge and into St. Olaf's Chapel. They were soon evicted, not for money changing in the temple, but for brawling and using bad language. Across the channel, London brokers were later banned from the Royal Exchange for rowdiness, and the English brokers migrated to the coffeehouses on a narrow street that became known as Exchange Alley.

In 1611, Amsterdam built a columned arcade modeled after the Royal Exchange of London (founded in 1566) and used this facility for over two centuries, even though the trading arena was an open air courtyard.

Soon after the Amsterdam Bourse opened in 1611, 300 brokers were operating for the benefit of the public. Admittance to the trading floor was free. Only beggars and children were banned. Using weapons or striking with the unarmed fist was forbidden. The beadle of the Bourse rang the bell (*een clockxken*) to close trading and collected fines from those that didn't hear or wouldn't quit.

The brokerage business was so lucrative that many brokers became very wealthy. However, there weren't any customers' yachts on the Zuider Zee. The business soon attracted discount brokers, making things much more competitive. The small investor was pursued with investment plans allowing purchase of stock in installments. Blocks of 20 shares, called *regiments,* were normally traded, but smaller purses were accommodated by mini-shares called *ducatons.*

In 1835, the original building was torn down and the exchange wandered about for 10 years, much as the New York Stock Exchange did in the same period after a disastrous Manhattan fire. The Amsterdam Bourse even had a brief stint in a wooden building in front of the Royal Palce, but that didn't last long. In 1845, a new building was built (no roof of course). The governors finally broke with tradition by roofing it in the 1870s. In 1913, commodity trading and stock trading were separated for the first time, with the current exchange placed into use for stocks.

Seventeenth-century Amsterdam was the financial center of the world. The first bank was founded in 1609 and lent money almost exclusively to the United East India Company. The Dutch West India Company was founded in 1621 to trade with the east coast of America and the west coast of Africa. The government developed a variety of debt instruments. Annuities and perpetual bonds were among the innovations. The market was active and volatile. The United East India Company paid large dividends, and the stock price doubled in a year. In 1683, speculators were treated

FIGURE 2–3
Amsterdam Bourse (1611–1835)

Note the open central courtyard where trading occurred and the water flowing under the structure. Stocks were traded by outcry in pits.

to the world's first stock split. Each share of United East India stock was replaced with 10.

The oldest stock certificate in existence today is held by the Amsterdam Exchange and dates to 1606. The businesslike contract has blanks for the stockholder's name, the amount paid, and the date of the agreement. On the back of the certificate, in handwriting, is an accounting of dividends paid in either cash, commodities, or both. The stockholder owning this certificate had received 379 pounds of pepper at 16 pence per pound for one of his dividends.

Windhandel was banned in 1610 but continued illegally until 1689 when it was legalized and taxed—an elegant solution to a decree that couldn't be enforced. By that time, traders were trying to play both sides of the market. The optimists were termed *Liefhebbers* (lovers) and the pessimists were *Contramineurs* (counterminers).

The first stock market book was written by Don José de la Vega in 1688, and he described the activity of the Amsterdam stock-jobbers as "double dealers." His description of the stock market is as applicable today as it was then: "A touchstone for the intelligent and a tombstone for the audacious."

CHAPTER 3

MANHATTAN—THE PLACE WHERE WE ALL GOT DRUNK (1609)

Although Giovanni da Verrazano was credited with being the first white man to discover Manhattan Island (1524), its history as a financial center really began with the visit of Henry Hudson in 1609.

While Verrazano was an Italian sailing a French vessel, Hudson was an Englishman commanding a Dutch ship of the United East India Company. His mission was to find passage to the Pacific Ocean, and he had already failed twice while under contract to the Muscovy Company.

The United East India Company had been commissioning explorations for both a northwest and northeast passage to China. Hudson was hired to pursue the course followed earlier by Sir Hugh Willoughby. Like Willoughby, he reached Novaya Zemlya before his crew mutinied and made him reverse course. Since it was still early in the season, Hudson headed west, ending up in Delaware Bay.

Hudson's ship, the Half Moon (*Halve Maen*), was flat-bottomed, two-masted, less than 60 feet long, about 80 tons' burden, and designed for the Zuider Zee. However, when Hudson sailed into New York harbor, the Indians were very impressed, variously describing it as a huge canoe, a large fish, or a floating house. Whatever it was, it contained *Mannitto,* "the great or supreme being," come to dispense judgment on the natives for their sins.

Runners on the Brooklyn shore spread the word from Harlem to Hoboken, describing a gorgeous godlike man in a red coat all glittering in lace on the front stoop of the house. The Indians prepared their choicest foods of dog meat and maize bread and, with an ample supply of green tobacco, paddled out to greet Mannitto.

The Indians taught Hudson how to fill a bowl and smoke the tobacco plant, which was unknown to Europeans. The natives were dressed in furs and feathers with copper necklaces, and a flourishing spot market in commodities soon was in operation with maize, beans, and tobacco being traded for beads and knives.

The Indians' strong impression of this first meeting has been passed down as legend among the Delaware tribes. Bishop Heckewelder, a Moravian missionary, recorded it in 1818.

According to the legend, Hudson produced a gourd from which he poured liquid into a cup. This he drank, then refilled the cup and handed it to the first chief. The latter smelled it and passed it on to the next Indian—thereby delegating responsibility—who also passed it on, until it had almost made the entire circuit, whereupon a warrior jumped up, lectured the tribe on discourtesy and the possible consequences, and, in a fit of bravery, bid farewell to the group and drained the cup.

The brave staggered, fell, and was soon sound asleep. The chiefs had begun to mourn him, when he jumped up proclaiming how well he felt and asked for more. Soon the others followed his example, and in a short time all were intoxicated. In the universal language of inebriety, a common denominator had been found. Thereafter, the Delawares and the Mohicans called the island on which the revels had been held *Manahachtanienk,* which means in the Delaware language "the place where we all got drunk." The white abbreviated it to Manhattan.

The name seems fitting in light of three centuries of subsequent developments and the many robber barons and fortune hunters that roamed the streets of lower Manhattan thirsting for wealth and drunk with the success of financial dealings.

By 1650, the town of New Amsterdam, a small village of 800 residents, had one of every four buildings devoted to the sale of alcohol in the form of inns or taphouses.

An American Indian teacher by the name of Joe Saddleback was later quoted as saying: "We taught the white man to smoke. I'm sorry we did that. The white man taught us to drink. He should be sorry that he did that!"

CHAPTER 4

FINANCE BY LOTTERY (1612)

The only sure way to make money without risk is to conduct a lottery. You collect the money, take your percentage, and make the random selection of winner or winners for the money that remains.

Distribution of wealth by chance or lot is probably prehistoric in origin. It precedes the Christian era because the Bible mentions Moses allocating Canaan by lot to the tribes of Israel (Numbers 26:55–56). We know Roman soldiers cast lots for Christ's clothing, and the Emperors Nero and Augustus awarded property, slaves, and houses by lot.

The profit motive was introduced into gambling or casting of lots in Venice during the 16th century, using them as a form of taxation. Venetian merchants, and those in Florence and Geneva too, distributed the tickets and held the drawings.

Francis I of France established a government *loterie* in 1539. It became vital to France's fiscal policy when the French people, revolted by the unrestricted spending of their monarchs, refused to pay more taxes.

The English held lotteries to subsidize the American colonists. The colonies then picked up on the idea and authorized lotteries to finance the construction of churches and schools, bridges, roads, lighthouses, and ports.

The Jamestown Colony, founded in 1607 in Virginia, was subjected to every form of adversity. Income was nil, and the merchants groups that organized the settlement found it increasingly difficult to support the colony. In the spring of 1612, the Virginia Company petitioned the king for relief and was granted a new charter empowering the company to conduct one or more lotteries. Tickets were sold in the large cities of England, and the first drawing in the summer of 1612 met with widespread approval. Two of the first three winning tickets were held by Anglican churches. By 1620, the lotteries provided about half of the ongoing expenses of Jamestown, but without warning, the House of Commons ordered an end to the sale of tickets and presented another blow to the struggling colony.

England was awash with lotteries in the 17th and 18th centuries, both government and personal, with virtually everyone selling tickets. The colonies observed this and instituted their own lotteries. George Washington was a devoted player of the lotteries that sprang up in the 1760–1800 period and sponsored the Mountain Road Lottery in 1768 to build a road across the Allegheny Mountains to the Ohio River. Just before his death, Thomas Jefferson attempted to dispose of Monticello by lottery in order to pay his debts.

Alexander Hamilton, our first secretary of the treasury, who started many of the U.S. fiscal policies, wrote a small treatise on "Ideas for a lottery." According to Hamilton, to be successful, a lottery had to be easily understood by the prospective ticket buyers so as to present "fewer obstacles between hope and gratification." The second recommendation is for low-priced tickets: "Everybody, almost, can and will be willing to hazard a trifling sum for the chance of considerable gain . . ."

Congress tried in 1776 to support the revolutionary troops by lottery but was unsuccessful in raising the $1 million sought. Some states were able to pay their troops after the fact by conducting lotteries. Federal Hall in New York City, site of our first government, was built by lottery. An attempt to fund the building of Washington, D.C., by lottery failed.

Private lotteries were outlawed by the middle of the 18th century, leaving the field to government and education. The University; of Pennsylvania, Columbia, Yale, Princeton, and Harvard held lotteries in the 1745–1765 period; with over 300 more college lotteries in the first half of the 19th century.

Early lotteries disbursed 85 percent of collections. Drawings were conducted by randomly selecting all tickets while a simultaneous drawing from a mixture of "blanks" and "fortunates" determined the awarding of prizes. By 1815, all towns of 1,000 population or more had a lottery broker. These dealers were the forerunner of underwriters for stock sales. They organized the lottery, guaranteed the sales, and conducted the drawing. Broker networks covered the country, and their handling of bank notes, promissory notes, and all types of currency led to the founding of banks. John Thompson was a lottery ticket salesman who founded First National Bank of New York City in 1863 and was a founder of Chase National Bank, chartered in 1873.

Another interesting sideline business known as *insurance* was set up to accomodate those without the full price of more expensive tickets. Where ticket drawing was extended over a longer period, the odds changed and speculation increased as to when the undrawn winners would appear. Bets were accepted by ticket sellers on which numbers would be drawn the following day, and the insurance "rates" or odds were published daily in the newspapers.

A person holding a yet undrawn ticket might wager that his ticket would be paired with a "blank." If the ticket drawn was a winner, then the side bet was disregarded as "insurance." If the ticket drawn was a loser, then he received something from the side bet.

These abuses led to reform drives, and by 1840, 12 states had anti-lottery laws on the books. One of the last states to outlaw the lottery was Louisiana, and by 1889, the Lousiiana State Lottery was the largest private lottery with annual gross receipts of $50 million. In 1890, use of the federal mails was banned to lottery operations, and without promotional means, the Louisiana lottery died.

That is the way it stayed in the United States, with some exceptions, until 1964 when New Hampshire established the first state-sponsored lottery of modern times, and now all the states are rushing to this source of revenue.

Various other forms of the lottery include bingo, sweepstakes raffles, pools, and so on. Sweepstakes beat the federal mail law by not requiring a purchase, using gentle persuasion to sell their product to raise the money for prizes. Some states have outlawed the sweepstakes specifically.

The government conducts a land-lease lottery by offering monthly drawings for oil and gas leases. "Tickets" are $10 and winners are allotted a lease that can be sold to a broker or oil company. Lease payment is 50 cents per acre per year and must be deposited in advance. If no lease is awarded (drawn), then rent is returned. Odds are not normally as good as in state-operated lotteries.

The Irish Sweepstakes pays out over $500 million per year. Numbers randomly selected are matched with a horse race. It is illegal everywhere except Ireland, but it thrives. In Britain, 300 million per year is bet on football pools. During World War II, Russia issued lottery tickets with each bond sold, and recently a Bulgarian State Lottery had as the prize a two-room apartment in Sofia.

CHAPTER 5

TIGER BONES (1613)

By 1600, trade between Western Europe and the Orient was flourishing, and a number of companies were organized to capitalize on the trade and to seek a shorter route to reach that trade.

The English East India Company was founded in 1600 on the equivalent of $400,000 capital. The United East India company (*Vereenigde oost-Indische Compagnie*) was started in 1602 with 73 directors based in Amsterdam with a stock subscription worth $1 million. The Dutch East India Company was a money-making concern, averaging 18 percent yield to its shareholders until 1632 when 12.5 percent became the guaranteed rate. Hudson was exploring for the Dutch East India Company when he discovered Manhattan Island. The company prospered until 1799, when it was dissolved.

The merchants were the motivation and financial support for most of the exploration. In 1613, a group of 13 merchants in Amsterdam hired Adrian Block to explore the area discovered by Hudson, particularly to assess the possibility of fur trading with the Indians, with the idea of developing a monopoly. Block's subsequent reports and maps became the basis for a charter issued by Holland for the New Netherland Company formed in 1614.

In 1613, Adrian Block set sail for America in his ship, the Tigre. Arriving in the fall, Block built four huts on an Indian trail following the spine of the island, at the lower end (where Broadway now connects Trinity Church with Bowling Green), and prepared to winter there. The Tigre, anchored on the west shore of Manhattan, was acccidently set on fire, burned to the water line, and sank. Block showed his versatility by cutting timber on the island and building a second ship of some 44.5 feet, named her the Restless,

FIGURE 5–1
Map of New Amsterdam after 1653.

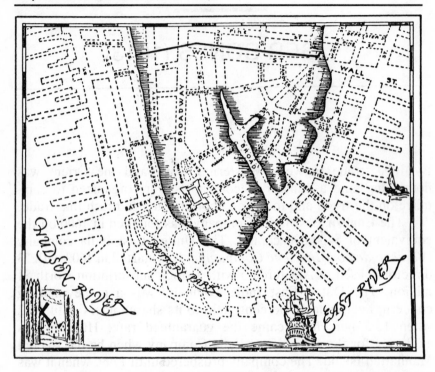

Note line of wall just north of present day Wall Street. Also note canal that was filled in 1674 to form Broad Street. Superimposed on the original shoreline is a more recent map showing the amount of land reclaimed from the sea.

and explored the rivers of New York and New England as far north as Cape Cod, leaving his name on Block Island.

Three centuries later, in 1916, workers excavating beneath the intersection of Dey and Greenwich streets turned up some flame-charred timbers, later identified as belonging to the Tigre. These now reside in the Museum of the City of New York. In 1613, the shoreline was at present-day Greenwich Street on the west and at Water on the east. The industrious Dutch reclaimed two city blocks on either side of the island, filled in the canal that runs under Broad Street, and doubled the land area of Manhattan below Wall Street.

In 1967, an excavation near Dey Street turned up a 17th-century breech-loading swivel deck gun. On the removable breechblock is the monogram "VOC" (Veneenigde Oost-Indische Compagnie) and an "A" above representing the Amsterdam chapter of the company. Since all activity on Manhattan after 1614 was conducted by the Dutch West India Company, the cannon obviously belonged to the Tigre. In 1614, Block had been sued by the Dutch admiralty for loss of the ship's cannon.

The 1967 excavation was in preparation for construction of the World Trade Center that now dominates the New York skyline. Since the center was to be built on landfill that once had been part of the Hudson River, excavation had to proceed carefully to keep the Broadway area from collapsing and further exploration for Tigre relics has been postponed.

In 1970, the World Trade Center opened for business, and work was completed in 1973. Today the twin towers shelter some 50,000 workers and 80,000 visitors each day.

Housed on the site in the World Financial Center are offices of Merrill Lynch, the world's largest brokerage firm. In 1982, Merrill Lynch created an investment product called Treasury Investment Growth Receipts (TIGRS), pronounced "tigers." This is a derivative of United States Treasury Bonds where the semi-annual coupons have been stripped for other investment use and the remainder of the security is sold as a zero coupon bond to the investor. This gives an investor the chance at a high quality government security not directly offered.

Isn't it ironic that under the building lies the skeleton of the first investment in Manhattan, known as "The Tigre," while the building houses the skeleton of one of the latest investments, known as a TIGR?

CHAPTER 6

THE SHORT SALE OF MANHATTAN (1626)

In the spring of 1621, while the Pilgrims were building their first permanent houses at Plymouth Plantation, the constitution of the Dutch West India Company was being approved at the Hague. The charter called for exclusive trade on the coasts of America and Africa. Subscription of stock began immediately; 7 million guilders were collected by September 1623.

By 1624, the company was functioning with a colony at Fort Orange (Albany) and eight men on Manhattan. The first colonization of Manhattan came the next year, and Peter Minuit was the first director general in 1626.

Minuit was an honest man and a capable administrator. During his tenure, the 300 citizens trebled their exports, while Minuit dealt fairly and peacefully with the Indians. Minuit built Fort Amsterdam near present day Bowling Green, and then he negotiated the purchase of Manhattan Island. There is some doubt about the Indians that showed up to conduct the sale being the rightful owners of Manhattan. In fact, there is doubt that any Indians resided on the island at that time. If these doubts are true, the Indians sold something they didn't own to the out-of-towner, much as other natives would do with the Brooklyn Bridge 300 years later. The agreed purchase price was 60 guilders, in beads and trinkets, at a time when a guilder was considered to be worth 40 cents (pence), thus the figure of $24 that made the history books.

Now the general opinion is that Minuit got the best of the deal, particularly when you consider that the entire 22 square miles for $24 could be compared to $622.29 per square *foot* paid three centuries later for the corner of Nassau and Wall. But let's consider what over 300 years does to money before jumping to conclusions. First let's set the record straight on the demeaning phrase, "beads and trinkets." Beads made from clam and snail shells had served as money among the Indian tribes for nearly a century before the white man's arrival. It had limited sources, required a constant amount of labor to produce, was difficult to counterfeit, and in general served as a stable currency for trading between whites and Indians. It stayed in use for nearly two centuries after the whites had arrived in America.

Next let's look at 60 guilders (or $24) and see if the Indians had made a good or bad deal. One way to begin is to consider the investments available; Holland had a perpetual government bond that paid 8 percent annually at that time. Perpetual means that it has no maturity date—no redemption—and continues to pay 8 percent indefinitely. There are a few of these still in circulation today.

If we could continue to reinvest the interest at the same 8 percent rate and allow the investment to compound for 363 years (1626 to 1989) then the $24 would have turned into $122,196,000,000,000. That means that the Indians would have bankrupted Holland some time ago and now could cover their short position by repurchasing Manhattan Island with 363 years of improvements. Not a bad deal!

Had the Indians sent smoke signals to the Amsterdam Stock Exchange, which opened for business in 1602, to pick up some perpetual bonds or, better still, bought 60 guilders worth of Dutch East India stock, they would have received dividends averaging 18 percent until 1632 and then a fixed yield of 12.5 percent until the company was dissolved in 1799. By 1799, the investment would be worth $58,360,100,000 and any further investment at 4 percent or better, compounded quarterly, would beat the perpetual bond.

Either way, the Indians scalped (figuratively) the white man based on the future value of the $24 received. Selling the rights to something you neither own nor use is an investors dream. Other parcels were sold to the Dutch patroons by other tribes along the Hudson River. There was never any lodging of complaints by the Indians, nor any bragging by the Dutch. If there were grievances, the Indians compensated themselves from the settlers livestock. All in all, a good business transaction for all parties concerned.

CHAPTER 7

TULIPMANIA (1637)

The tulip acquired its name from the Turkish word for *turban*. The tulip was introduced into Western Europe around 1550. The first bulbs came from Constantinople, where the flowers were already in favor. At first, the tulip was a commodity of interest only to the wealthy, who sent to Constantinople for their collections and paid extravagant prices for them.

The Amsterdam Stock and Commodity Exchange underwent a decade of speculative frenzy beginning in 1607. By 1620, tulip bulbs were commanding huge prices, and the general public was attracted. Botanists were busily mutating the bulbs, and the principal interest was in displaying the results.

In a natural state, the tulip is basically one color, with large leaves and a long stem, but when weakened by cultivation, the variegations are infinite. The petals become paler, smaller, and more diversified in hue, and the leaves turn a softer green. The weaker it gets, the more beautiful it becomes, until at its best, it can barely be transplanted and is difficult to keep alive.

By 1634, tulips were such a rage among the Dutch that ordinary industry became neglected. Virtually everyone became involved in raising, buying, and selling tulip bulbs. Prices for the more exotic varieties ran as high as $2,000 per bulb. There was one instance of a single bulb being traded for a successful brewery.

Futures contracts on commodities had been trading for over 500 years by this time, but a new product that we know as options was introduced, allowing the small, poorly financed speculator to join in the madness. Sellers sold bulbs they didn't own to buyers that pledged money they didn't have, and both sold options to others. This was *windhandel,* or trading air, in its finest form!

The ignorance of foreigners to the tulip craze provided tragicomedy relief. One sailor delivered some goods for a merchant and was rewarded with a fine red herring for his breakfast. Spotting an onion nearby, he slipped it into his pocket and made off for the docks to enjoy his herring. The onion turned out to be a Semper Augustus, worth about 280 pounds sterling. When the merchant caught up with the sailor, he was putting the finishing touches to breakfast. The sailor's reward for this indiscretion was several months in prison.

Another traveler, an English amateur botanist who should have known better, came across a tulip root in the conservatory of a wealthy Dutchman and began a detailed dissection. The owner soon appeared and ask if he knew what he was doing: "Peeling a most extraordinary onion," replied the visitor. It's an Admiral Van der Eyck, moaned the Dutchman. "Thank you," replied the traveler, "Are these Admirals common in your country?" A mob led him to the local magistrate, where he was invited to join the sailor.

By 1636, the frenzy was at a peak. People of all grades turned property into cash and cash into flowers. Foreigners were pouring money into Holland from all directions. Price inflation for the necessities was raging. Small towns, where there was no exchange, had tulip notaries. The principal tavern was usually selected as the showplace, and hundreds attended the auctions.

But all "bubbles" come to an end, and by 1637, the market was "toppy." No one displayed tulips any longer—everyone traded them, and the prudent withdrew from the markets. Soon the floating supply of money and "greater fools" had been soaked up, and a dealer found that he had no buyer for an expensive bulb in his inventory. This panicked the other brokers, and contracts were defaulted. Prices dropped quickly to less than 10 percent of their peak value, and litigation began. The practice of law became a growth industry, the economy staggered, but the Dutch had established a love for tulips that persists today.

CHAPTER 8

COLONIAL CURRENCY (1650)

The colonists brought very little money to America. What resources they had were turned into implements and supplies in order to be self-sustaining in the new world. England was involved in a civil war and unwilling to supply the colonies with money. In addition, England forbade the minting of money in America.

Barter became the instrument of trade, and it worked well until the colonies became so prosperous that a more convenient method of conducting trade was needed. Being given a cow to build a house was fine if values were comparable and if you had some use for the cow or could trade it for something needed.

Virginia adopted tobacco as a currency in 1619, and the poor discovered that with a little effort they had the next best thing to a money tree. Overproduction induced inflation, and food crops such as corn were neglected. This continued until 1645 when the policy was overturned.

Nails were used for a short time because the labor required to produce them was constant, keeping their value stable, and they were compact and convenient to handle. However, resale value of homes became less than the cost of nails for building a new one, so owners took to burning their homes to recover the nails. This presented a fire hazard, and the Virginia legislature finally had to supply the nails for new homes in order to stop the practice.

Bullets had a more lasting success, and furs came into significant use after John Jacob Astor began actively trading with the Indians.

The currency in place when the colonies arrived, dating back before 1535, was wampum. The word was an abbreviation for *wampumpeage,* which meant "white string." Variants of the word were *peak, sewant, roanoke.*

FIGURE 8–1
White Wampum and the Pillar Dollar (actual size)

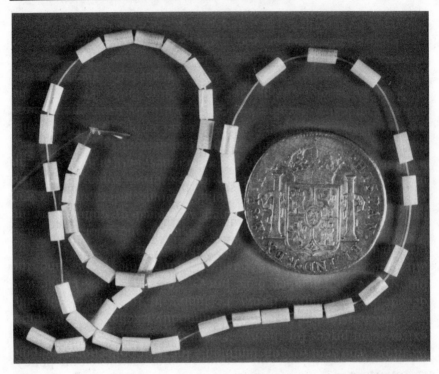

Note pillar with scroll that was source of dollar symbol ($).

The original manufacture of wampum was by the Iroquois Indians, who strung the hearts of white periwinkle shells and used the constructs in virtually all financial transactions. It also had a mystic quality; the shell was supposed to stop nose bleeds, and legend had it that shell collection could be made by "fishing" with the dead as bait.

In 1553, the French explorer Jacques Cartier wrote about the Iroquois of Montreal: "When an Indian has incurred the death-penalty or they have taken some prisoners in war, they kill one and make great incisions in the buttocks and thighs, and about his legs, arms and shoulders. Then at the spot where this esnoguy (snail) is found, they sink the body to the bottom and leave it there for ten to twelve hours. It is then brought to the surface and the above mentioned cuts and incisions they find these shells, of which they make a sort of bead, which has the same use among them as gold and silver with us.''

Since much trading was done with the Indians, it was easy for the colonists to adopt their system. The value of wampum was stable, as it took one hour's labor from a squaw to isolate the heart of the shell, form it into a quarter-inch cylinder, drill the center to form a pipe, and string it. The production of wampum did not exceed the production of goods and services, so it served as a stable currency for over two centuries. In 1735, the Campbell family set up a factory in New Jersey and mass produced wampum for over a century.

Tables of value were posted in each colony, relating any currency commodity to wampum and the English shilling. For example, a six-foot string of white wampum was worth one bullet, and both were worth one shilling.

The purple heart of the clam shell was also used for wampum and, being rarer, commanded a value twice that of the white. However, it was easy to counterfeit, so transactions were often specified in white wampum (taxes, for example).

The first use of coins in America came from a variety of nations trading with the colonies. The Spanish eight-reale piece was minted in Mexico City as early as 1536, contained good silver, and was widely accepted by the colonists. In 1652, New England minted some shillings with trees on the face (oak, pine, willow), in defiance of English law. Politics and bribes smoothed over the indiscretion later. The mint eventually closed, due to a lack of good silver and the universal acceptance of the Spanish coin as the basic unit of currency.

The pieces-of-eight reales minted in Mexico were different from those made in Spain by the reverse side. This consisted of a crown above a shield, flanked by the "Pillars of Hercules."

The Pillars of Hercules are the two rocks that guard the straits of Gibraltar, placed by Hercules, according to Greek mythology. On the coin, the pillars are wound with a scroll, and the symbol was adopted, simplified, and placed in use to represent the dollar ($). The *pillar dollar* was accepted as legal tender by the General Court in 1672. It was rated as six shillings to the dollar and remained the basic unit of American currency for nearly two centuries.

Eight feet of white wampum was equal to one dollar and usually used for change, but eventually the dollar became chiseled into eight pie-shaped wedges, each one reale (known as one *bit*). A shave and haircut cost two of these bits. When stock trading began in 1792 on the waterfronts of New York, the prices were quoted in bits or eighths. That tradition carries forward to this day.

While president, Thomas Jefferson proposed a decimal system with the pillar dollar as centerpiece. U.S. coins in a variety of denominations were minted, and in 1853, the pillar dollar was outlawed by Congress.

CHAPTER 9

PEGLEG'S PALISADE (1653)

In 1637, William Kieft became the third of four Dutch director-generals for the West India Company in New Amsterdam, and although he was industrious, much of his rule saw the colony in turmoil.

To raise revenue for his projects, Governor Kieft demanded tribute of the Raritan Indians on the grounds that the Dutch provided for their defense. The tribe refused to pay, and Kieft promptly raided their settlements (thereby demonstrating the need for defense), killing and destroying crops. The Raritans thought that was unfair, since they always paid for everything they got from the Dutch, so they returned the raiding favor by wiping out the outlying settlements and confiscating the livestock.

So, on the morning of March 31, 1644, a proclamation was nailed to the wall of Fort Amsterdam calling for a barrier to be erected at the north of the settlement, sufficiently strong to prevent the straying of cattle and to protect from the Indians. The notice warned all interested persons to be available on April 4 for the prosecution of this work. Apparently, the cattle guard consisted of untrimmed trees, felled at the edge of the forest and piled together to form a barricade running from the Hudson River to the East River.

In 1647, the last Dutch governor, Peter Stuyvesant, arrived to rule New Amsterdam with a firm hand.

Stuyvesant had lost a leg fighting the Portuguese and had been fitted with a peg leg before his appointment as governor.

Stuyvesant negotiated a peace with the Indians, and the colony prospered under his rule. However, he continually cast a nervous eye at the English colonies of New England and kept New Amsterdam on alert for attack by the English.

To thwart the vulnerability of attack from the north, Stuyvesant decided in 1653 to replace Kieft's barricade with a stronger defense. Stuyvesant intended to tax the 800 residents for construction costs, but they objected that it was the responsibility of the Dutch West India Company to provide for their defense. A compromise was effected where a tax on beer and wine collected by the company was diverted to provide for construction of the wall.

Bids were called for, and a future pirate by the name of Tom Baexter won the contract and was paid the equivalent of $1,300 in "good wampum."

The palisade was 180 rods, or approximately 3,000 feet, in length and was constructed from 12-foot posts of 6-inch diameter with the tops sharpened. The base was sunk three feet into the ground. Later, five bastions or artillery mounts were constructed and a "screen" added 10 to 12 feet of extra height to the wall. The plans included a sloping breastwork, a ditch, and a parade ground.

The wall was built, but an assault was never attempted. Instead, the English came by sea, and when their ships finally appeared in the harbor in 1664, they were welcomed with open arms even as Stuyvesant tried futily to incite the Dutch to fight.

By 1685, the wall across New "York" had fallen into disrepair. Large sections were down. British Governor Dongan bought the lots north of the wall through an agent, had the street along the wall surveyed to enlarge his holdings by 64 feet, and then started selling his questionably acquired property. He was well ahead of his time with this demonstration of insider trading.

In 1699, the Common Council petitioned his excellency to remove the wall as an obstructing nuisance and to utilize the stones of the bastions for the new city hall. By this time, the street was well defined, the city concentrated on the tip of the island, and the stage set for its development as the financial center of the world.

When New Amsterdam was taken by the English, Peter Stuyvesant was given safe passage back to Holland, where he was drummed out of the West India Company. He returned to New York in 1667 to live the remainder of his life among the people and gardens that he loved. He brought fruit trees from Holland and planted them on his country bowerie (farm) near present-day 13th Street and Third Avenue. One of the pear trees lived for 200 years and, encircled by a fence, became a landmark where the streets cut Stuyvesant's estate. In 1867, a runaway horse collided with a rig turning the corner, knocking it into the fence and tree, with both going down. A scion was immediately planted within the same railing. The remnants of Stuyvsant's tree reside with the New-York Historical Society. Legend has it you can still hear his peg leg and cane echoing down the canyons of Wall Street as he inspects his palisade.

CHAPTER 10

THE GREAT WAMPUM
CORNER (1666)

To become wealthy, a person has to have at least one major opportunity in his life, and it must be acted on boldly. Frederick Philipse had two, and he capitalized so well on both that he became the wealthiest man in New York and was known as "The Dutch Millionaire" before the end of the 17th century.

Philipse was born Vréderyck Felypsen in Holland in 1626 and emigrated to New Amsterdam in 1647. He worked as a carpenter for Peter Stuyvesant on the Old Dutch Church and before long was made the official carpenter for the Dutch West India Company. This included duties as builder and consulting architect. There was a wall to be built!

In 1662, Philipse married the widow Margaret Hardenbrock De Vries, who had a large heritage from her late husband's fur trade in which she, personally, had carried pelts to Europe, establishing the first packet line between the old and new worlds. She ruled the ships and sailors with an iron hand and had plenty of capital at her disposal. She had the money and Philipse knew what to do with it—he bought wampum!

Wampum had been the official currency for trade with the Indians since 1635. They wouldn't accept gold or silver coins for their animal furs, and the colonists didn't have much in the way of hard money anyway. The ratio of sewant (wampum) to beaver stayed fairly stable because there was a limited supply of each.

But by 1650, the shells had started to depreciate and Governor Peter Stuyvesant was faced with the same dilemma that still occurs today: how to fix the value of depreciating currency to stop price inflation. He first set the price at six white beads to one Dutch stuiver (approximately 50 per dollar or 2 pence to each stuiver). This made the exchange ratio at about three per penny—a penny was useful then.

Stuyvesant tried to get the West India Company to send him coins to replace the shells and stop the devaluation. The company refused because "it was beyond our means."

The New England traders exacerbated the situation by creating a monopoly on Long Island clam banks, bringing 25 percent more wampum to the New York marketplace. By 1658, the value had gone from 6 to 8 beads per stuiver. In 1659, it went to 16 to a stuiver and the effect was disasterous.

The widow and her money showed up at just the right time for Frederick Philipse. Anticipating a rise in the value of wampum, Philipse bought and "planted" (buried) whole "hogsheads" (large barrels) of wampum. By 1663, the price began to rise because Philipse had cornered the market. Those that had made contracts to pay in sewant could find none and had to approach Philipse and take his price. By 1666, the value had gone from 16 beads per stuiver to 3 per stuiver, and Philipse had quadrupled the family wealth. Later, John Jacob Astor bought wampum by the bushel to support his fur trading with the Indians, and the Philipse corner had a similar secondary benefit.

Next, Philipse went into real estate in a big way. Governor Stuyvesant had granted him city lots earlier. Now Frederick changed his politics and loyalties to the English conquerors, and the British government supplied him with extensive tracts of land. And, of course, he bought from the Indians. He soon had a long strip of land on the Hudson, north of Manhattan, stretching from present-day Yonkers to Tarrytown. The piece of land was large enough to be officially termed a *manor,* and he was titled as a lord. He built a castle on the manor and a Dutch church in 1699 that is now the oldest in New York State. John D. Rockefeller restored the manor early in this century. Yonkers was originally Philipseborough; Tarrytown was Fredricksborough.

To reach his lands more conveniently, Philipse built the first bridge, Kingsbridge, across the Harlem River in 1693. One of his industries involved silver and iron mines along his Hudson properties.

In 1691, Philipse extended his trade to the pirates' settlement in the Indian Ocean. Having bought a French prize ship from Captain Kidd in 1691, he employed Samuel Burgess, Kidd's ex-crewmate, in 1693 and sent him back to Madagascar to trade with his old colleagues. Burgess carried clothing, liquor, and naval supplies to the pirates and slaves back to New York. His wife having died in 1691, Philipse remarried in 1692 to the daughter of the wealthy Olaff Van Cortlandt and therby augmented his fortune even further.

Philipse continued to prosper until he died, owning large segments of the business district on and near Pearl Street, fleets of seagoing vessels, and one third of Westchester County. He served as city surveyor and alderman and on the governor's council for 20 years.

Like others that would follow to work the narrow path known as Wall Street, Philipse was less than an admirable character. However, America's first tycoon exhibited the bold, rugged spirit that was needed to settle and develop the industrial possibilities of this vast new land.

CHAPTER 11

THE PIRATE AND HIS CHURCH
(1696)

My name was Robert Kidd, when I sailed, when I sailed
My name was Robert Kidd, when I sailed
My name was Robert Kidd, God's laws I did forbid
And so wickedly I did, when I sailed

I'd ninety bars of gold as I sailed, as I sailed
I'd ninety bars of gold as I sailed
I'd ninety bars of gold and dollars manifold
With riches uncontrolled as I sailed

To execution dock I must go, I must go
To execution dock I must go
To execution dock will many thousands flock,
But I must bear the shock—I must die!

Ballad popular at the time of Kidd's hanging

By 1689, William Robert Kidd was an experienced member of a French-English crew on the Blessed William in the Caribbean. Because of the animosity between France and England, the non-French crew members stole the ship, made Kidd the captain, and turned to privateering against the French. While Kidd was accepting plaudits on shore from the English colonists on the island of Nevis in the West Indies, his crew took off with 2,000 pounds of booty in the hold, leaving Kidd temporarily short of resources and making a statement about honor among thieves.

Governor Codrington rewarded Kidd with a recently captured French vessel renamed Antigua, and Kidd set out in pursuit of the Blessed William. He learned his shipmates were headed for New

FIGURE 11–1
Trinity Church (1698)

Trinity Church and the wall coexisted for slightly more than one year. The landgate (opening) was at Broadway. In 1693, 10 feet of the south side of the street was paved. The unpaved portion of Wall Street served as a parade ground.

York, a pirates' haven at that time. New York City was hospitable to pirates because their gold stimulated the depressed economy.

Kidd arrived early in 1691 to find his ship sold and the crew gone. He lay claim to one of the French prize ships taken by his old crew, eventually selling it to Frederick Philipse for 500 pounds. He immediately married the wealthy Sarah Bradley Cox Oort, just days after Sarah was widowed for the second time. Kidd became the third of four husbands that she was to outlive.

From 1691 to 1696, Kidd lived the life of a colonial burgher, living off his wife's estate, which included a mansion on Pearl Street and the first husband's house on the north side of Wall Street. Some of Mrs. Kidd's possessions were sold in 1694 to buy a pew in Trinity Church, the new Anglican church that was soon to be built. As construction of the church progressed, Captain Kidd loaned his block and tackle for setting the stones in the foundation.

Kidd had retained the Antigua, and in 1695, he sailed for England, intending to wage war on the pirates working the Indian Ocean. He received a privateering commission and left London for New York in the Adventure Galley in February 1696.

Arriving in New York in May 1696, Kidd used the summer to provision the ship and select his crew. Since the village was in the throes of a depression, more than enough men were willing to share his adventure and its lure of profits.

In September 1696, the Adventure Galley set sail for the Cape of Good Hope and the French buccaneers to be found in the Indian Ocean.

As the Adventure Galley sailed away from the dock at the east end of Wall Street, Trinity Church began to rise from the graveyard at the head of Wall. The Dutch had used a large tract of land just inside the wall, along the Hudson River, as a burial ground, and now the Anglican Church had selected a site on this ground just off the Indian trail (Broadway) that ran from the wall to the tip of the island.

The charter for the church was granted by William III of England, and a squat little wooden building with an oversize steeple emerged for its opening services on March 13, 1698. The church boasted 20 pew-holders, with the name of Captain William Robert Kidd adorning number 16. Kidd was never to sit in that pew. At that time he was half a world away, socializing with his old shipmates in a pirate settlement near Madagascar.

While Kidd and his friends were enjoying their spoils, the most powerful economic institution in England, the prosperous East India Company, was falling on hard times due to war and pirating. Kidd soon emerged as a symbol of its troubles, and he was to be made an example.

Kidd returned to the West Indies in April 1699 and found out he wasn't welcome in New York. However, he proceeded to Long

Island in June, sailing back and forth near Gardiners Island, waiting for negotiations to clear his arrival in New York. He was finally made to believe that if he appeared in a Boston court, he would be pardoned, so he sailed there July 3 and was taken into custody.

In February 1700, Captain Kidd began his last voyage back to England to stand trial May 8, 1701. On May 23, 1701, William Robert Kidd stood on a short ladder with a rope around his neck and when the hangman kicked the ladder away, the legend began.

Estimates of Kidd's fortune ran to 400,000 pounds, and Kidd himself had offered bribes of 20,000 pounds to his antagonists to gain his freedom. Rumors of hidden treasure have persisted to this day, and much of the east coast has been dug up in pursuit of that treasure.

Meanwhile, Trinity Church prospered, with pews reserved for the mayor and other dignitaries. In 1754, the church gave some of its land for the erection of King's College (Columbia). The building was financed by lottery, and one of its students when the revolution broke out was Alexander Hamilton. After his duel and death in 1804, he was buried in Trinity Churchyard.

In 1776, under British occupation, the church was burned, along with much of the city. The chief suspect was Nathan Hale and the Liberty Boys. In 1788, the ruins were cleared and the grounds served as a park and social center until the new church was completed in 1790.

The second church, built in the Gothic style, was more imposing than the first and served the congregation until 1839. It then became necessary to destroy it, when the heavy snow of that year damaged the roof. George Washington attended church there while presiding in New York.

The present structure was dedicated in 1846, and its age-darkened presence stands guard at the head of Wall Street. Its beautifully paneled bronze doors were donated by William Waldorf Astor, grandson of John Jacob Astor. These doors are open daily, and the clock and chimes mark progress in the Wall Street canyons.

CHAPTER 12

THE MISSISSIPPI COMPANY (1719)

John Law was born in 1671 in Scotland and went to work in his father's counting house when he was 14. For three years, he studied the banking principles of Scotland, demonstrating an extraordinary proficiency in mathematics. When he was 17, his father died, and Law set out for London to see the world.

Because of his mathematical bent, he was very successful at the gambling houses and was soon earning a comfortable living. He was also a favorite of the ladies, and his dual interests led to a duel with a Mr. Wilson. Law had the bad fortune to shoot Mr. Wilson dead and was tried and sentenced to die. Law managed to escape and fled to the continent, where he resumed his interest in gambling and in Amsterdam developed a skill for speculation.

Earlier, Law had proposed a "land bank" with paper credit to the Scottish authorities, but the parliament had rejected it. In France, Law became friends with the Duke of Orleans, and after Louis XIV died, Law's friend and patron became regent for the seven-year-old heir to the throne. The Duke was very interested in Law's schemes to restore the credit of France. France had a 3 trillion livre national debt, and with revenues of only 145 million and expenses of 142 million, the debt was rapidly increasing.

On May 5, 1716, a royal edict allowed Law to establish a bank. He made his notes redeemable in the coin current at the time the notes were issued. Since the government was continually depreciating the coins by reducing the precious metal content, Law's notes became more valuable than the coins. Branches of his bank were established all over France.

Law proposed to the Duke to establish a company that would

trade with the Mississippi River territory of America. The area was supposed to abound with precious metals. The Mississippi Company was subsequently incorporated in August 1717. Capital consisted of 200,000 shares of 500 livres each. After an initial success, the government extended trading rights with the French East India Company, and the Mississippi Company created the Company of the Indies with 50,000 new shares.

Law's house in the Rue de Quincampoix was beset by eager applicants for shares. Stock-jobbers moved in, and the narrow street became an open air market. House prices increased dramatically. A cobbler who had a stall there was given 200 livres per day to lease his building. A hunchback became wealthy by lending his hump to be used as a writing desk. Eventually Law moved his corporate offices to the Hotel de Soissons, which had elaborate gardens where trading was conducted. About 500 small tents and pavillions were erected where crowds continually moved in and out.

Speculation soon reached fever pitch with prices fluctuating 10 to 20 percent per day. An extensive holder of stock, being ill, sent his servant to sell 250 shares at 8,000 livres each, which was the latest quote. Upon arrival at the hotel, the servant found the price had risen to 10,000 livres. The difference realized was 500,000 livres (about $200,000), which the servant coolly transferred to his own use. After delivering his master's money, he departed the same evening for another country.

Law's coachman made enough money to set up a carriage of his own and gave notice of his intended departure. Law begged him to find a replacement of equal ability. The coachman soon appeared with two men, telling Law to make his choice, with the understanding that he would employ the one not chosen.

Early in 1720, the paper pyramid began to crumble. The warnings of parliament that too much paper money would sooner or later create bankruptcy had been ignored for some time. Paper currency had been issued without regard to hard assets or precious metals to support it. The regent, Duke of Orleans, continued to issue paper, and Law didn't attempt to stop him.

The crunch came when a prince was denied more Indian stock at his own price, and so he converted his paper into specie and carted it home in a wagon. Stock-jobbers began to quietly turn their paper profits into jewelry and silverware. One man by the name of Vermalet converted 1 million livres into gold and silver coin, packed it into a farmer's cart, covered it with hay and cow dung, and disguised in a dirty peasant's blouse, drove his precious load into Belgium.

Gold and silver withdrawals were soon restricted in an attempt to shore up paper value, and Gresham's law came into force (good money is forced into hiding by bad money). Coins disappeared, but no one wanted to accept paper money, and trading came to a halt. The government made it illegal to own coin, jewelry, silverware, and other assets.

Shares of the Mississippi Company declined, and the tales of immense potential wealth were no longer believed. The government conscripted 6,000 of the poor of Paris and marched them through the streets as if they were on their way to Louisiana to mine gold. Two thirds of them "escaped," sold their shovels, and returned to the slums.

By May 1720, the notes in circulation had a face value of 2,600 million livres, while the coin minted was less than that amount and the notes were soon depreciated accordingly. Stock of the Mississippi Company fell below the 500 livre par value, down from 40 times par at its peak, and riots became commonplace, directed at anyone connected with the original scheme.

John Law was relieved of his duties and soon left the country, eventually being accepted again into England, after having been pardoned from the earlier murder conviction.

Law was soon back on the continent finishing out his life, much as he started, in the gambling houses of Venice, with much reduced means. His grand scheme was a shambles, but he is credited with establishing paper money as a viable form of currency.

CHAPTER 13

SOUTH SEA BUBBLES (1720)

The South Sea Company was formed in 1711 by the Earl of Oxford, with the intention of restoring public credit in England. A group of merchants agreed to assume the army and navy debt (10 million pounds of debenture), and the country in return would tax imported goods to produce a 6 percent interest return per annum. The company was granted a monopoly to trade with the south seas— particularly the east coast of South America where gold and silver mines existed in Mexico and Peru. It was thought that Spain would allow free trade with its colonies.

Philip V of Spain, however, had no intention of allowing free trade, and the South Sea Company languished until 1717, when it was proposed that the capital be expanded to 12 million pounds by new issue of stock. Parliament debated this proposal, and the company name was continually before the public. The stock was in demand, and the directors brought before parliament a plan to pay off the national debt. The debt was some 30 millions pounds. The agreement called for 5 percent interest until 1727 when the debt could be redeemed by the legislature.

Exchange Alley underwent a speculative frenzy. When the company expansion bill was introduced on February 2, 1720, the stock was selling for 130 pounds. The next day it was 300 and rising.

The bill was two months progressing through the House of Commons, and rumors about company prospects abounded. The stock rose about 400 but settled back to the 330 level when the bill was passed by the House of Lords on April 7. The legislators were deeply and personally involved by this time. Everyone became a stock-jobber, and Exchange Alley was blocked with human traffic.

In this atmosphere, a number of other schemes were introduced. Some of them lasted a couple of weeks, but their sudden appearance and disappearance earned them the title of *bubbles*. There were nearly 100 different projects, including some outrageous ones: There was a proposal to make lumber out of sawdust, one to trade hair, one to make a wheel for perpetual motion, and one to extract silver from lead.

The most preposterous proposal was submitted by an unidentified entrepreneur under the prospectus of "a company for carrying out an undertaking of great advantage, but nobody to know what it is." The required capital was 500,000 pounds in 5,000 shares of 100 pounds each. The subscription required a down payment of only 2 pounds per share and guaranteed a return of 100 pounds per annum (100 percent on par or 5,000 percent on the shareholder equity).

The prospectus stated that all would be explained in one month and that the other 98 pounds would be due at that time.

The subscription office opened at 9 o'clock, and when it closed at 3 o'clock, there had been 1,000 shares bought and deposits made. Not being as greedy as his clients, the underwriter promptly closed the doors forever, departed the same evening for the continent, and was never heard of again.

On June 11, the King issued a proclamation fining any broker that bought or sold the illegal bubbles, and on July 12, all bubble companies were dissolved. Eventually the parliament passed the Bubble Act, which forbade the issuing of stock certificates by companies. It was not repealed until 1825.

Meanwhile, the South Sea directors were propping up the price of the stock and opening up their books for a fresh subscription. After a temporary low of 290, the stock soon advanced to 340. On April 21, a 10 percent dividend was declared and a second new subscription was made. The men were meeting their brokers in the taverns, and the ladies doing the same at the milliners. In the Alley, prices changed so rapidly there was as much as a 10 percent spread from one end of the street to the other.

On May 28, the stock was selling at 550, and about two thirds of the government annuitants had traded their state securities for those of the South Sea Company. Early in June, it reached a price of 890, and the nobles and government officials began to appear in the Alley to sell. On June 3, the price fell to 640. The directors sent their agents into the Alley to buy and the price stabilized around 750. By the beginning of August, the stock had passed the 1,000 level, which was the apex of the bubble.

The directors did their best to maintain the price by jawboning, but the stock dropped over 100 points even as they met the public. By September 12, the price was down to 580 and in a steady decline that ended at 135.

Eventually the legislature persuaded the two super-companies—the Bank of England and the East India Company—to absorb some of the South Sea Company and provide some stability to its finances. One by one, the directors were brought to trial in early 1721, had their estates confiscated, and some were locked in the Tower of London, depending on their role in the mischief conducted.

Sir Isaac Newton, the mathematical genius that made significant contributions to science, was caught in the bubble and parted from some 20,000 pounds. This caused him to lament: "I can calculate the motions of heavenly bodies, but not the madness of people."

PART 2

BIRTH OF A NATION (1776–1835)

CHAPTER 14

FINANCIER OF THE REVOLUTION (1776)

Robert Morris came to Philadelphia from Liverpool in 1747 and began work in a countinghouse. By 1754, he was a partner in Willing, Morris, and Company, a leading colonial merchant with commercial ties to England. When the fighting started, Morris became a super patriot, unlike other merchants. He was a leader in the Pennsylvania assembly, chairing the council when Franklin was absent.

As a member of the Continental Congress, he personally arranged the procurement of vessels, munitions, and naval armaments using the Willing, Morris channels and collecting his broker's commission.

Morris signed the Declaration of Independence, the Articles of Confederation, and was chairman of the congressional committee on finance.

When finances for the Revolution (continental currency) collapsed, Morris was appointed superintendent of finances on February 20, 1781. Morris was a hard money man without any hard money and with a losing cause to finance.

Morris's solution was to establish the first United States bank, which was named the Bank of North America. This facility was to support the patriot cause, lend money to the government, and operate the business on a hard money basis. As fine an idea as motherhood and apple pie, but hard to attain.

Morris went after three sources of capital: First, he made the bank a place of deposit and asked all prominent patriots to subscribe any specie they had. As you might expect, this source produced little cash. It's one thing to be patriotic, quite another to be foolish with your money.

Next, Morris took the commodities that had been donated by the states in the absence of money and traded these for hard money in the West Indies. This also produced little cash.

The third approach was to seek a loan of specie from a foreign country. France saved the rebel cause by a loan of $500,000 to be redeemed by tobacco. A French fleet brought over $200,000, and the Bank of North America opened its doors in January 1782.

Morris himself was one of the principal subscribers and further strengthened the bank by using his personal credit to back notes, guaranteeing as much as $1.4 million at times. Using every financial trick at his disposal, and to a tune of personal criticism and abuse, he financed the Yorktown campaign, which ended organized British military power in the colonies.

Meanwhile, the states refused to accept their obligations to produce revenue. Congress was impotent, and in despair and disgust, Morris resigned January 24, 1783, accompanied by an uproar by the people and abuse from the press. Nobody else would take the job, so he was prevailed upon to retain office until the army was paid and demobilized. A loan from the Netherlands, secured by John Adams, allowed Morris to leave office in September 1784 with public credit high, and his own fortune intact.

In postwar politics, Morris supported the federalist cause— calling for a strong central government—and Washington asked him to serve as secretary of the Treasury. Morris declined, but served in the U.S. Senate from 1789 to 1795.

Along with Washington and others prominent in the government, Morris speculated heavily in western land after the war. Western land at that time was Pittsburgh, Buffalo, Cleveland, and so on. He also was a partner in a large tract of the wilderness that was to become the site of Washington, D.C.

Not foreseeing the Napoleonic wars and the collapse of the American economy, which had been built on a pyramid of credit, Morris became land poor with cash flow problems. No one had money to buy from him, and he needed cash to pay taxes and interest on his loans.

Morris's financial empire collapsed even as L'Enfant, the French architect, was building him a palace in Philadelphia. He retreated to a country estate, where in February 1798, he was arrested on the charges of a small creditor and incarcerated for three and a half years in a debtor's prison.

Released in August 1801 under the federal bankruptcy law, Morris lived his last five years in a small house in Philadelphia.

Gouverneur Morris (no relationship) had served as a deputy superintendent of finance under Robert Morris and secured for Robert's wife an annuity that provided his only support until his death. He died a forgotten and much pitied man in 1806.

CHAPTER 15

FATHER OF HIS COUNTRY
(1789)

In June 1775, Colonel George Washington, a country gentleman from Virginia, passed through New York on his way to take control of the colonial troops in Cambridge, Massachusetts. A year later, General Washington was back in New York preparing for the next British strike. The Liberty Boys had removed all the guns from the abandoned Fort Amsterdam, and the HMS Asia, lying in the harbor, fired on New York City. The chief casualty was to Samuel Fraunces, who lost the roof of what was to become a famous tavern.

Washington had deployed his troops in Brooklyn and Manhattan, and when news of the Declaration of Independence came, Washington ordered it read to all the troops. He personally read it to the men gathered in the fields (present City Hall Park). The Liberty Boys hurried down Broadway to drag the leaden statue of George III, "darling of the people," from its pedestal. It later supplied 40,000 bullets to be fired back at the King's redcoats.

But the rebels were outnumbered, undersupplied, poorly trained, and operating in a populace with mixed sympathies. With 30,000 British professionals advancing on New York and a major battle under way on Long Island, George Washington showed his strategic skills by evacuating General Putnam's entire army from Long Island by boat under a shroud of darkness and harbor fog. George certainly knew how to cross a river. Manhattan was a British stronghold until the end of the war, but by November 25, 1783, the last of 10,000 royalists had fled the city, and as the last regiment of redcoats left, George Washington, Governor Clinton, and a few hundred tattered veterans rode down the battery to

FIGURE 15–1
Federal Hall in 1789

View is north on Broad of building on Wall. Before renovation, structure was City Hall, built in 1699 using materials from the wall.

cheering throngs. The general and his troops had been camping where Central Park would be built, waiting for the departure of the English.

The procession formed at the Bullshead Tavern in the bowery, and proceeded down Broadway to Bowling Green. Nine days later, in the long room of Sam Fraunces Tavern (with the roof restored), Washington bid an emotional farewell to his troops: "With a heart full of love and gratitude, I now take leave of you. I most devoutly wish that your latter days may be as prosperous and happy as your former ones have been glorious and honorable. I cannot come to each of you, but shall feel obliged if each of you will come and take me by the hand."

Washington left that same night by barge from Whitehall to return to Mount Vernon and civilian life.

When Washington went back to his life as a gentleman farmer, the Continental Congress went to work in New York. City Hall, the site of present day Federal Hall at Wall and Broad, was vacated for their lodging and use. City officials moved to the corner where the New York Stock Exchange now resides.

A month after ratification of the Constitution, in July 1788, work began on rebuilding Trinity Church and tearing down City Hall to make room for the new Federal Hall. L'Enfant, the French architect, designed the building and planned the future capital of the United States, then known as National City.

In March of 1789, the building was ready and Congress assembled. On April 6, Congress elected George Washington president and John Adams vice president. The city now prepared for the inauguration, and Washington started his journey from Virginia.

On April 23, 1789, flags and banners adorned Wall Street from the rapidly rising second Trinity Church to the East River. Washington arrived at Elizabethtown Point in New Jersey by 9 A.M., but it was 3 P.M. before cannon and bells welcomed his state barge to the Wall Street wharf on the East River. Thousands lined the street as he was escorted to his lodgings in the Franklin House on Pearl Street. The inauguration was to take place one week later.

At noon April 30, 1789, the presidential procession had started, even as Congress debated how they should receive Washington and the form with which he would be addressed. The procession turned onto Broad from Pearl and proceeded to Wall, where Washington and his escorts went into the Senate chambers of Federal Hall.

Washington soon stepped out onto the balcony fronting onto Wall Street, and the cheering throng in the street below went wild. There was a moment's pause as the dignitaries took their places, and then Chancellor Robert Livingston administered the oath. The official proclamation "Long live George Washington, president of the United States," was followed by the thunder of artillery and renewed cheering.

Across the street, Alexander Hamilton watched from the window of his house, and in the crowd was Washington Irving, then six years old. Irving had been six months old when Washington followed the retreating British into New York in the fall of 1783.

Federal Hall gave way to the United States Customs House, which in turn became a United States subtreasury. Today the Federal Hall museum occupies the site of so much of New York's political history. In front of the building, in the approximate space where George Washington was sworn in as the first president, stands a statue of the father of our country. The statue was created by J. Q. A. Ward and placed 100 years after the evacuation of the British. Ward also did the sculptures in the pediment of the New York Stock Exchange.

On July 27, 1790, President Washington made his last official visit to Wall Street in his ornate coach, with all the trappings of dignity, to sign a treaty with the Creek Indians, whom the young nation had been battling in the south.

The treaty was signed, the peace pipe was smoked and passed, and after Congress adjourned on August 30, Washington boarded the same magnificent barge used on his arrival and took his permanent leave of the city.

CHAPTER 16

ALEXANDER HAMILTON'S STOCKS (1790)

Six weeks before the Boston Massacre, the Battle of Golden Hill was fought in New York City. The hill was located where John and William streets now intersect, and the rebel cause was defended by the Sons of Liberty, or Liberty Boys, as they were known.

The Liberty Boys would be termed terrorists today as they ran amok for the five years preceding the battles of Lexington and Concord. One evening in 1775, this fun group showed up at King's College (now Columbia) to take the royalist-minded president for an unrequested midnight ride. While the president was hurdling the back fence of the institution, in his nightshirt, an 18-year-old student was eloquently addressing the mob from the front porch of the presidential residence, buying time for the president's hasty departure. The student was Alexander Hamilton.

Hamilton was active in the rebel cause, writing pamphlets that kept the populace stirred. At the outbreak of hostilities, Hamilton enlisted in an artillery company and was with Washington on Long Island. The battle for Long Island was a disaster, and the continental army escaped only through the masterful efforts of three people: Washington supervised the East River crossing; Mrs. Murray, a Quaker lady, delayed the pursuit by inviting General Howe to dine—it was still a civilized war at that point—and the rebel general, Putnam, was led out of the maze of the city by a longtime Manhattan resident named Aaron Burr.

Burr and Hamilton both had distinguished war careers, and when the Revolution ended, both studied the law and established offices in the Wall Street district. However, their politics and life-styles were in conflict. Hamilton and Washington believed in a strong central government, while Jefferson and Burr felt that concentration of power was dangerous and advocated states' rights.

Hamilton was appointed the first secretary of the treasury and set out to restore the country's flagging credit. The $2 million in bills of credit voted by the Continental Congress in June of 1775 had managed to get the republic through the war, but the continental currency collapsed in May 1781. Two months later, only hard money was accepted and the expression "not worth a continental" was created. In its six years of existence, the money depreciated to well less than 1 percent of the face value. Government attempts to prop it up by decree, requiring it to be honored at the face value, failed.

The money had no real backing through hard assets or taxation, and now the young country's economy was a shambles.

Hamilton proposed redemption of the continental currency at face value in bonds, which prompted a speculative frenzy— especially among the politicians, who hired boats and started working the Atlantic Coast to buy up the paper.

Jefferson argued against this proposal because only the middleman speculators would benefit from this measure. Why should the federal government pay more for the money than the people who would be redeeming the bills? Hamilton countered that to establish its credit, a government had to keep its word.

Having filled their personal portfolios with continental currency, in 1790, members of Congress took up the issue, which consisted of both the redemption provisions and the assumption of the states' debts. Several of the southern states objected to having their lesser obligations subjected to the inevitable level: taxation that would bail out their northern neighbors.

Hamilton needed one more vote in the Senate and five in the House to get the continentals redeemed. Jefferson had just returned as secretary of state from Europe, and he was lobbying to have the capital moved from Wall Street to the Potomac River in Virginia, near his birthplace. Although each disliked the other, a trade was effected, and Jefferson delivered the votes to pass the bill. Senator William Maclay of Pennsylvania, a wry observer and writer of the time, noted: "Speculation wiped a tear from either eye!"

The measure called for redemption at the rate of one cent of specie for each dollar in face value, and the paper issued, called *stock* in the English fashion, was really 6 percent bonds. Some $7 million of continental paper was retired, and the bonds became an instrument of trade. The same people who lost on the continentals now had to furnish the tax that paid the bond interest.

Commodities had long been traded on the docks of New York at the foot of Wall Street, and now the government bonds were added to the auction lists. An interest in the paper alone soon emerged, and a group of brokers decided to specialize in the bonds, signing an agreement to trade this government issue for the public and among themselves.

Meanwhile, Hamilton and Burr continued their competition and animosity. Hamilton chartered the Bank of New York and kept competing banks from being chartered. Burr outmaneuvered him with the Manhattan Company. Burr tied Jefferson in electoral votes in 1803, even though they belonged to the same party and Burr had been the vice presidential candidate. Hamilton liked neither but influenced a runoff election that selected Jefferson. Bored with the vice presidency, Burr ran for the New York Assembly, and Hamilton personally saw to his defeat.

The end result of this continuing struggle between two strong-willed individuals was a written insult by Hamilton, followed by a challenge from Burr. A duel was fought at Weehawken Heights, New Jersey, on July 11, 1804. Hamilton died the next afternoon, and Burr's career effectively ended. The vice president of the United States had shot the first secretary of the Treasury, and the country lost the services of both men. Hamilton was buried in Trinity Graveyard at the head of the street where he spent most of his adult life.

CHAPTER 17

THE BIG BOARD AND THE BUTTONWOOD TREE (1792)

At 1 P.M. April 30, 1789, the carriage of General George Washington proceeded north on Broad Street, through massed throngs, to his appointed inauguration at the Federal Hall on Wall Street. His six escorts included Major Leonard Bleecker.

Leonard Bleecker was a personal friend of Washington, standing with him as witness to the surrender of Cornwallis at Yorktown on October 19, 1781. Leonard Bleecker was also the first broker to sign the Buttonwood Agreement on May 17, 1792. This document is considered to be the beginning of "The Big Board," or New York Stock Exchange today.

New York had a market in meal and slaves at the foot of Wall Street as early as 1752. In 1776, France lent the colonies $10 million at 5 percent interest, redeemable in tobacco, and when Hamilton convinced Congress to redeem the war debt with an issue of bonds, they were first traded with other commodities by auction at the waterfront market.

The action in bonds soon led a group of 24 brokers to specialize in "stock," and they began to meet regularly under a buttonwood tree on Wall Street. The agreement signed in 1792 called for doing business for customers at not less than 1/4 percent and to give preference to each other.

In 1793, the Tontine Coffee House was completed, and the buttonwood brokers joined other merchants in meeting inside. The coffeehouse was built by 203 subscribers paying $200 each to share in ownership. One of these owners was John Jacob Astor, who was well on his way to wealth as a fur merchant. The tontine plan is Italian in origin, with shared ownership eventually reverting to the sole property of the last survivor.

The stock brokers met in an upstairs room and ran an auction on some seven issues, once each day, while comfortably seated. Thus, their membership was termed a *seat*.

Trading proceeded in government "scrip" until a formal constitution was written and adopted in 1817. This group took the name of New York Stock Exchange Board. Of the original 24 buttonwood signatories, only three remained. Not only was Leonard Bleecker still active, but also another Bleeker was now a member and eventually became president of the board from 1827 to 1829.

In 1819, the yellow fever epidemic forced the exchange out of the financial district and initiated a period of years of wandering, including a brief sojourn in a room at the rear of Leonard Bleecker's home.

The development of railroads and the discovery of gold led to intense speculation, and a number of securities exhanges sprang up during the middle years of the 19th century. By 1848, each had been absorbed by the Big Board. In 1869, a merger was effected with the Open Board, and their brokers celebrated by carrying their vice president, in his official chair, to Delmonicos, where they wined and dined him and deposited him (still in his chair) on the floor of the Big Board. The New York Stock Exchange was reconstituted.

In 1865, the Big Board moved to Broad Street, near Wall. The building cost nearly $2 million, and the architect, James Renwick, had previously designed St. Patrick's Cathedral. He also was consultant for the Morris Canal.

In 1899, property on both sides was purchased and an expanded facility was planned. The old building was razed and the new structure completed in 1903, and with some modification, it has been in use since that time.

Today the Big Board is responsible for over 80 percent of the dollar volume of securities traded in the United States. There are 1,375 seats that can be bought or sold like any other commodity. The initial 24 members grew to 533 during the Civil War, and then the merger with the Open Board raised strength to 1,060. In 1928, membership limits were raised to present levels.

Seats that were originally added at $400 began trading freely after the Civil War, near the $2,000 level. In 1929, prices for seats were near $600,000 and receded to under $100,000 during the depression years. Today prices are at new record levels, near $1 million.

Bleecker and the buttonwood tree have both returned to dust, and the membership of the Big Board is no longer seated. The auction has given way to continuous trading, but capitalism is alive and well 200 years later at the corner of Broad and Wall.

CHAPTER 18

BURR'S WATERWORKS AND BANK (1799)

A little more than one mile north of the original settlement on Manhattan Island was a deep pond fed by subterranean springs. This pond had outlets to both the Hudson and East rivers, which essentially cut the island into two parts. The Indians camped around the pond, fishing and duck hunting, and discarded clam and oyster shells on a point of the lake the Dutch soon named Kolck Hock (i.e., Shell Point). The English pronounced *Kolck* as collect and the pond became known as "the collect."

As New Amsterdam grew, cattle were herded through the wall and up to grazing fields called the commons (now City Hall Park) or farther on to the shores of the collect. Eventually, farmers were enticed to live in the wilds by being given a stocked bouwery (bowery or farm) by the Dutch West India Company under a rental agreement that required payment of 80 pounds of butter each year and return of the original stock after six years. Soon there was a string of farms from the wall to the collect, and one of these boweries become Peter Stuyvesant's retirement manor.

As the city grew, so did the need for water, and just before the Revolution it was proposed that water be piped from the collect throughout the city. The Revolution stopped the planning, but in 1799, after several years of yellow fever epidemics, Aaron Burr proposed to the state legislature that the Manhattan Company be formed to supply pure water to the residents. Burr had an ulterior motive in mind.

In 1784, the third bank to begin operations in the United States was the Bank of New York. It monopolized the financial activities of the state of New York. Alexander Hamilton was a director,

FIGURE 18–1
The Manhattan Company Reservoir (1799)

The reservoir stood on the north side of Chambers Street, between Broadway and Centre. Building was in the Egyptian style, topped with a bronze Aquarius. Water was gravity-fed to lower Manhattan through buried log water pipes.

wrote the constitution, and used his political influence to keep other banks from being chartered. Hamilton also headed the citizen committee for a waterworks, and Burr wrote the charter for the Manhattan Company, stating an intent to provide New York City with a pure water supply. The yellow fever siege created an urgency that led to quick approval by the state assembly.

The Manhattan Company charter contained a clause stating that surplus funds raised by the public offering could be used "in any other monied transactions or operations not inconsistent with the constitution and laws of this state or of the United States. . . ." Thus was born Burr's Bank of the Manhattan Company.

The stock was capitalized at $2 million, and the company directors met on April 11, 1799, and quickly decided on the springs and wells of the collect as a water source. By May 6, a superintendent was appointed and negotiations were under way for land to be used for wells and reservoirs. By the end of the first year, six miles of wooden pipe had been laid, serving 400 houses.

The pipe consisted of pine logs, one foot or more in diameter, with a three- to five-inch hollow in the center of the logs, tightly fitted and buried in the ground. Water was moved to the reservoir by a horse-powered pump located at the corner of present-day Centre and Reade. The octagonal reservoir made of stone and mortar stood on Chambers Street, held 132,600 gallons, and was adorned by the figure of Oceanus, adopted as the company seal.

Pipes were laid following Broadway down to the battery, with lateral lines down the side streets to both rivers. The system when completed was 25 miles long and served over 2,000 houses, supplying the city for 43 years. In 1803, a steam engine replaced the horse at the pump.

The company drew up a schedule of fees for the use of water, and lead pipes were used for extension of the service into homes or a courtyard, where often the entire neighborhood was supplied.

The system was gravity fed from the reservoir down the spine of the island (Broadway) and to lower levels east and west to the East and Hudson rivers. As the pipes were laid farther from the reservoir, the opening was narrowed to increase water pressure at the tap.

Much of the 690,000-gallon daily capacity was used to fight the many fires that plagued the city in the early 19th century. About 150 wooden fire hydrants were placed throughout the city, but often the firefighters would drill a hole directly in a water main to procure water. Large wooden plugs were used to close these taps after the fact, and the term *fireplug* entered the language.

By 1805, the system was well-established, but the collect had become a festering eyesore. It was decided it should be filled in by leveling the hills surrounding it. On the south slope of Bunker Hill was the Bayard family vault. Peter Stuyvesant's wife had been a Bayard. The hill was condemned and the remains of the Bayards were moved.

The city rapidly outgrew the water supply, and the directors had no interest in expansion, as banking had long ago become the primary business. The Manhattan Company soon lost the water business to the city, and by 1875, only four families were still using company water. By 1885, the last four users were gone, but the reservoir was maintained, and a certain amount of water was pumped onto the ground each day to validate their charter. In 1900, the legislature amended the charter so that water service was no longer necessary, leaving banking the sole business of the Manhattan Company, as Burr had planned a century earlier.

The Bank of the Manhattan Company prospered until 1951, when Chase National Bank proposed a merger. However, the original Manhattan Company charter called for unanimous approval by all shareholders in order to be acquired. It took four years and a new president of Chase, with an imagination, before the Bank of Manhattan Company, with $1 billion in assets, acquired Chase National Bank with its $6 billion. The press heralded it as a case of Jonah swallowing the whale!

Hamilton and Burr finally settled their differences by their famous duel in 1804. The pistols used in the Burr-Hamilton duel had an active history. Their owner, Colonel John B. Church, Hamilton's brother-in-law, bought them in England. Church himself had fled England after a duel in 1779 and used the pistols for a duel conducted in New Jersey in 1799. His opponent was Aaron Burr.

Burr and Church were both directors of the Manhattan Company, and Church had slandered Burr. This occurred the day before opening the Bank of the Manhattan Company. After close of the first day's business, the principals enacted their duel in Hoboken. Business came before pleasure even then. A button was knocked from Burr's coat; Church offered the *amende honorable,* and the matter was closed.

Three years later, the pistols were used again and Alexander Hamilton's son Philip was mortally wounded on the site where his father would fall two years later.

On July 11, 1804, the Church pistols were used for the last time at Weehawken by Alexander Hamilton and Aaron Burr. As the challenged, Hamilton chose and supplied the weapons and set the rules for the encounter. He chose 10 paces, rather than the customary 12 to 15. The closer distance favored the speed of firing rather than accuracy, and the weapons had a secret hair trigger mechanism.

Whether Hamilton set the hair trigger and who fired first is a matter of controversy, confused by the partisan witnesses. The facts are that both men fired. Hamilton hit a tree limb over Burr's head and in return took Burr's shot in the abdomen.

Hamilton died the following day. Both careers ended with the duel, but both their banks are prosperous today. The waterworks is long dead, but the hollowed-log water mains still turn up today in underground excavations of lower Manhattan.

CHAPTER 19

THE LANDLORD OF NEW YORK (1801)

During the Revolutionary War, the Duke of Hesse was paid 850,000 pounds per year by the English for the conscription of 29,166 soldiers to fight the war with the colonies. Parading up Broadway in August 1776, after its victory on Long Island, the Hessian contingent was followed by Heinrich Ashdour, riding a sutler's wagon.

Ashdour was a butcher by trade and had joined the soldiers in order to come to America. In New York, he soon became a contractor of meats, impartially butchering both rebel and loyal beef. His success was relayed in letters to his younger brother, Jacob, in Wald Dorf, Germany, who shortly departed for London and his uncle's music business as an interim step. In 1784, Jacob arrived in America with $25 and seven flutes.

Jacob's first job was with a friend of his brother, as a baker boy, selling bread and cake in the streets. He changed the family name to Astor and was selling musical instruments by 1786. Two years later, he was John Jacob Astor and he had added furs to his enterprises.

It is generally assumed that Astor started his fortune from shrewd fur trading with the Indians, but there were plenty of shrewd fur traders operating in the century before Astor arrived, and none of them were able to accumulate the kind of wealth that Astor hoarded in the years 1801–2. Some $1.3 million went into his account at the Manhattan Company (Aaron Burr's waterworks and bank). The deposits were drafts drawn by Roderick Streeter of London, one of the largest dealers in precious stones in the world. There were no other banks in use by Astor, and the deposits ended abruptly in 1802. The legend stemming from these mysterious accumulations becomes facinating reading as told by Frederick L. Collins in his book *Money Town*.

The story begins with Captain William Kidd, who was a resident of Wall Street in the last years of the 17th century. After he was hanged for piracy in 1701, it was rumored that he had left buried treasure in the vicinity of New York City. Some estimates ran as high as 400,000 pounds, and Kidd himself offered to fetch some 20,000 pounds for his prosecutors during the trial.

After his capture in Boston, Kidd had handed his wife a note with the number 44106818 printed on it. A commission of British experts spent months in a fruitless search for the treasure.

The story moves forward nearly two centuries to 1892, when Frederick Law Olmsted, who had landscaped Central Park in New York City and Capitol Hill in Washington, took his children on a treasure hunt.

Olmsted had inherited an estate on Deer Isle, off the coast of Maine, and while digging in a cave, the treasure party found a cavity in the clay filled with softer earth that carried the impression of a box, complete with bolt marks.

Two years later, an astronomer visiting Olmsted calculated the latitude and longitude of the island as 44° 10′ and 68° 13′, which Olmsted's daughter recognized as near Kidd's mysterious 44106818. The astronomer noted that a slight error in time would account for the difference in calculated longitude.

This new information set Olmsted in motion with research revealing that a fur trapper, one Jacques Cartier, employed as part of Astor's network, had lived in a loghouse and worked the island at the end of the 18th century. After struggling for years on less than $500 per year, in 1801, a payment of $5,000 by Astor put the fur trapper into retirement. Astor's deposits in the Manhattan Company, never exceeding $4,000 per year, suddenly jumped to more than $500,000 in that same year.

His curiosity aroused, Olmsted learned that the last home occupied by Astor had been sold to a wrecking firm two years earlier (1893) and among the rubbish was a rusty old box. Olmsted shipped the box to Deer Isle, where it fit snuggly into the bolt holes of the clay. Partially obscured by the rust were the initials W.K.

However accumulated, Astor certainly knew what to do with

his $1.3 million bank account. He bought real estate. He never seemed to buy anything good. It was all swamps and rocky farmland. He bought large farms along Broadway and in the area that is now Times Square. Farms worth $20,000 brought $20 million a century later.

By the time of his death in 1848, Astor had made purchases of near $2 million and sales of just under $1 million. The net result was judged to be worth $500 million while still possessed by the Astor family in the 20th century.

John Jacob Astor bought from the financially troubled, and he bought from the wealthy. He bought Aaron Burr's 160-acre estate on Richmond Hill in 1804, just one month before Burr's duel with Hamilton. He took advantage of land-poor Trinity Church and its need for operating funds. The last Trinity Church built in 1846, at the head of Wall Street, with its clock and chimes marking financial progress on the street, has beautifully paneled bronze doors donated by the great-grandson of John Jacob Astor.

Astor leased land under the standard practice of the day. He rarely improved the land, but sometimes bought buildings, erected by the tenant, when the lease expired. Other times the improvements were confiscated. The tenant paid the taxes as part of the lease. He did foreclose some properties, but only when good business practice dictated that action.

Basically, he bought a commodity (land) that was rapidly becoming scarce, leased it, and held on tenaciously as time, inflation, and compounding multiplied his wealth. Before his death, he stated that his only regret was that he had not bought the entire island.

CHAPTER 20

OTHER PEOPLE'S MONEY (OPM) (1809)

Legend has it that Nathan Rothschild received advance notice of Napoleon's defeat at Waterloo in 1815. He then made a show of personally going onto the floor of the London Stock Exchange to sell consuls (English state bonds), giving the impression of a significant English defeat. The market broke sharply, and Rothschild agents quietly bought heavily in the depressed market. The next day official couriers brought news of the French defeat, and the Rothschild fortune was made.

The favorite version of this story attributes Nathan's "inside information" to courier pigeon. Another view has him personally riding out to the battlefield as an observer, with fast transportation waiting at the channel.

The story probably has some basis in fact, but less glamorous details detract from the story. First, price quotations for the days in question show less than 2 percent variation and no extremes in volume of activity. Short selling was banned in England at that time, so he would have had to work strictly with his own money and have a lot of it to make anything out of a 2 percent variation in price.

In fact, he did have a lot of money, but it was the result of other-people's-money (OPM).

The father of the Rothschild family and fortune was Mayer Amschel, who established himself as a rare coin dealer in Frankfurt after the French Revolution, late in the 18th century. One of his clients was William, landgrave of Hesse-Cassel and heir to one of the largest fortunes in Europe. Prince William's father had started the fortune by supplying Hessians to serve the British in the American Revolution, and William had extended it significantly.

Mayer worked his way into William's court by selling him the rarest coins at discount prices. With Napoleon overrunning Europe, Mayer placed his five sons in five countries, and the Rothschilds became banking agents, collecting from William's debtors while the landgrave went into hiding.

Napoleon had cut off William's sources for investment, so Mayer suggested that he buy consuls through his son Nathan in London. The prince reluctantly acquiesced, and some 550,000 pounds sterling reached Nathan for investment starting in February 1809.

Nathan was to buy consuls at an agreed price of 72, but the price was below that and dropping, so Nathan employed the money in his own interests. He bought cheap consummable commodities and smuggled the goods around the blockaded continent at dear prices through his brothers. He also speculated successfully in gold bullion, catching the rise almost to perfection.

William was continually calling for his consuls, but Napoleon's blockade was cited as the reason for nondelivery. By 1811, the price had dropped to 62 and Nathan began buying and delivering the prince's securities at the agreed price of 72. The Rothschild credit, fortune, and reputation were established, and wealthy clients rushed to align themselves with the Rothschild banking house. Waterloo was still four years away.

Another fortune begun with other people's money was a parlay conducted by Andrew Carnegie. His family came to America in 1848 by borrowing the passage. Andrew began as a 13-year-old to apply the time-honored principles of hard work, thrift, and discipline. He also discovered the principle of borrowed money.

By age 20, Andrew was working for the Pennsylvania Railroad at $30 per month. One day Carnegie's employer offered him 10 shares of Adams-Express stock that a friend wanted to sell. (In 1840, Alvin Adams began carrying parcels in two carpetbags between Boston and New York.) Not having any money to invest, Andrew asked the boss to give him a six-month installment plan to pay for the stock. He then went to a moneylender and borrowed the first installment at a high rate of interest. Next, his mother arranged a second mortgage on their home to help meet the repayment schedule. Eventually, the dividends on the stock and Carnegie's salary repaid all obligations.

Three years later, he managed a 12.5 percent interest in the Woodruff Sleeping Car Company and was given another installment schedule in return for promotion of the venture. This time he went to the bank, apparently used Adams-Express as collateral, and borrowed the first payment of $217.50. After that, dividends from the two properties covered the payments.

Three years after this, dividends from his first two investments were used to buy into Columbia Oil, and at age 28 his annual income was $42,260.67 (tax return) with only $2,400 as salary.

Other people's money (OPM) is a theme drummed into real estate investors. We recognize that a business or real estate needs borrowed funds, but we are hesitant to borrow for other investment purposes. We should recognize the equities markets as a business and fund our selections appropriately.

Failure is possible, as it is in a small business or in a house that we can't resell; but I would suggest that the risk—if properly managed—is no worse than any other form of investment.

CHAPTER 21

WATERED STOCK (1819)

"With his short position under stress, Uncle Dan'l
cranked the press."

After the War of 1812, Daniel Drew became a drover on the
$100 substitute fee paid his as a 15-year-old volunteer. He bought
and sold cattle on consignment by driving his herds from Putman
County to New York City. The city at that time was confined to the
lower end of Manhattan Island.

Like Drew, his cattle were lean and hungry and not known to
bring the best prices. However, that all changed when Uncle
Daniel put his sharp mind to work.

Heinrich (Henry) Astor had come to New York with the
Prussians during the Revolutionary War and was one of the city's
leading butchers. His younger brother was John Jacob Astor, who
joined Henry in America and traded his seven flutes into $25
million through the medium of furs.

Drew contacted Henry Astor and suggested that he meet him
north of town at the Bullshead Tavern (26th Street and Third
Avenue today). The night before meeting Astor, Drew camped at
Haarlem Village (125th and 3rd) and turned his cattle loose on salt
that he had purchased for the occasion. Carefully keeping the cattle
away from water, he drove the herd to the Bullshead and then
allowed them to take their fill of water just before Astor arrived.
The extra 50 pounds per head resulted in Drew concluding a very
profitable trade.

Daniel spent the next two weeks avoiding Astor and never was
able to sell to him again, but an interesting situation soon developed. Astor introduced Drew to one of his competitors, and Drew
sold him "watered stock." This led to a string of new customers

FIGURE 21–1
Daniel Drew

Courtesy of Brown Brothers Stock Photos

that were good for one sale each. Finally the word got around, and Uncle Daniel had to look for a new business.

His next venture was to become proprietor of the Bullshead Tavern located on the Lorrilard estate. Pierre Lorrilard was a cigar and snuff manufacturer and possibly the first American millionaire. He was at least the first to have the term applied to him by a newsman writing his obituary in 1843.

Since cattle buyers and sellers met at the tavern, it wasn't long before Drew was acting as a banker for them, which eventually led to an office in the financial district.

After a side trip into steamboat transportation, Uncle Daniel got interested in railroads and, in the panic of 1857, was able to work his way into the management of the New York and Erie Lake Railroad (Erie) by lending money to the line.

Soon Drew was manipulating the stock like a virtuoso. As an insider, he could create rumors that would move the stock in the direction he was playing. And the street recognized his talent by stating: "Daniel says 'up'—Erie goes up. Daniel says 'down'—Erie goes down. Daniel says 'wiggle-waggle'—it bobs both ways!"

During a period of expansion, Daniel secured a $3 million loan with $3 million in convertible bonds and 28,000 shares of unissued stock that was laying in the treasury.

Ignoring the fact that he was a director and treasurer of the line, Drew sold short. In those days, the short contract had an expiration date, and the securities didn't have to be delivered until that date. When it was time to fill the contract, Drew delivered the stock from the treasury and knocked the props out from under the market. Erie dropped from 95 to 47, and Drew bought back the treasury stock at half price. Drew had "watered" the Erie, just as he had "watered" cattle earlier.

Later Drew helped his protégés Jay Gould and Jim Fisk into the management of the Erie, and the three soon began a bear campaign on the stock. Their "bull" opponent was Commodore Vanderbilt, who soaked up every share offered by the tricky trio. Just when it appeared that the Commodore had cornered the market, the executive committee of the Erie (consisting of Drew, Gould, and Fisk) voted an additional 100,000 shares of the Erie and the printing presses began to roll. These were passed on to the Commodore at $70 per share before the ink was dry. Vanderbilt finally caught on and had an order out for their arrest, but they had "escaped" to New Jersey with 7 million of the Commodore's dollars packed in suitcases.

Eventually, the Commodore forced them to repay him, which Drew graciously accomplished by raiding the Erie treasury for the money. This led to Drew's ouster from the company and started him on the road to bankruptcy as he was forced to operate as a common "outsider." Drew said: "To specilate [*sic*] in Wall Street when you are no longer an insider, is like buying cows by candlelight."

Jay Gould once told a story about Drew, cited in *The House of Morgan* (Corey): "At one time, Drew went into a Methodist Church while a revival was in progress, and listened to a convert telling how sinful he had been, lying, cheating, and robbing men of money in Wall Street. Greatly interested, Drew nudged a neighbor and asked: 'Who is he, anyhow?' 'That's Daniel Drew,' was the reply.''

Today the Securities and Exchange Commission serves as watchdog over any dilution of stock. It does occur, but only with proper legal approval and with full disclosure to all shareholders.

This dilution may come from exercise of rights, convertible bonds, or new issue. When a company is in financial difficulty, often the debt holders are asked to take shares freshly created under court supervision as partial payment on the debt.

The "insider" problem still exists to some extent, to the small shareholders' detriment. Occasionally, the trustees will raid the treasury for "greenmail" to buy back shares held for potential takeover. This protects management, but the excessive price reduces book value and "waters" the share value. Possibly the time has come for the SEC to lock up the salt and turn on the electricity for us little investors, by approving offers made by management to raiders seeking a hostile takeover. Drew, Gould, and Fisk are long gone, but their memory lingers.

CHAPTER 22

MORRISON KENNEL (1835)

I've got a mule and her name is Sal
Fifteen miles on the Erie Canal
She's a good worker and a good old pal
Fifteen miles on the Erie Canal

We've hauled some barges in our day
Filled with lumber, coal and hay
And we know every inch of the way
From Albany to Buffalo.

The Erie Canal

Canals have been a means of inland transportation for centuries, and a canal connecting the Great Lakes with the Atlantic Ocean was proposed as early as 1724. In 1783, George Washington spoke in favor of developing the canal. In 1796, an incomplete canal connecting Lake Ontario to the Hudson River was opened.

Gouverneur Morris, who developed our coin system, backed the canal plan and chaired the Erie Canal Commission in 1810. DeWitt Clinton, later governor of New York, was a commissioner and led the long and difficult campaign to build the canal. Ground was broken in 1817, and the canal was opened to traffic in 1825.

The Erie Canal provided an all-water system from the Great Lakes to the Port of New York, establishing an outlet for the Midwest farming and industrial output. The growth of New York City was phenomenal, and the New York Stock Exchange was resurrected from a near death state of apathy.

When the Erie Canal opened, the newly constituted New York Stock and Exchange Board was operating out of the back room of broker John Warren's apartment. The trading list consisted of

FIGURE 22–1
The Morris Canal in 1868

This inclined plane at Newark, New Jersey, was 700 feet long with slope of 1 foot in 10. Jointed cradle carries boat to summit. Note toll booth at left on top of plane.

banks, insurance, and government issues. The Erie Canal ushered in the age of industrials, and active markets followed the railroad expansion. The first railroad stock listed for trading on the New York Exchange was the Mohawk and Hudson Railroad, which started trading in August 1830.

To illustrate the activity of that time, a typical day was January 25, 1830:

Stock	Shares	Price
United States Bank	31	117.25
Merchant's Bank	10	98.75
Delaware and Hudson Canal Company	75	87.5–87.75
Ocean Insurance	20	151
Union Insurance	50	103.5–104
Franklin Insurance	24	102.5
Fireman's Insurance	35	98
New York Gas Light Company	50	101
New York and Schuylkill Coal Company	170	102–104

The dullest day in recorded market history was March 16, 1830, when 26 shares of the United States Bank traded at 119, and 5 shares of the Morris Canal and Banking Company went for 75.25. It took only $3470.25 to finance all purchases on that day. Morris Canal—"Morrison Kennel," in Wall Street jargon—was to be the subject of the first speculation and "corner."

The term *corner,* as used in the American markets, connotes a monopoly of some commodity, stock, or other item. The person(s) cornered cannot usually escape, much as a person backed into the corner of a room.

However, corner—used as a noun—first appeared in American newspapers in the 1850s to describe manipulations in railroads, even though it seems to be rooted in the writings of Starkey of England in 1538, when he defined corner as: "Riches heaped in corners, never applied to the use of others."

The Morris Canal and Banking Company was planned in 1822 and authorized in 1824 with a charter for banking services and a plan for a 102-mile-long canal to connect the Delaware River at Easton, Pennsylvania, with the Hudson River at Jersey City, New Jersey. The bank was to provide money for other canals to be built.

The Morris Canal and Banking Company was named for the county it was to traverse, which had been named after the first colonial governor, Lewis Morris. Morris was the grandfather of Gouverneur Morris, who was graduated from King's College (Columbia) in 1768, was elected to the Continental Congress, and was assistant minister of finance under Robert Morris. Gouverneur drew up the decimal money system we use and coined the term *cent*.

"Morrison Kennel" was established with the blessings of the State of New Jersey and with public money from 20,000 shares issued at $100 per share. The books were opened in 1825, and the stock was the darling of Wall Street. Both Jacob Little and Daniel Drew cut their investment molars on the stock.

The canal was opened for traffic east to Newark in 1832 and extended to Jersey City in 1836. It was an engineering marvel with 28 locks and 23 inclined planes, which allowed it to negotiate the 914 feet of elevation between terminals. Its prospects for profits went up and down like the coal barges that navigated its water. In January 1837, the stock sold above "par" at 106, but the panic of that year carried it below 50. In 1833, it had sold even lower, and Daniel Drew approached John Ward, president of the New York Stock Exchange, about a "pool" to "corner" the stock. Drew thought that $100,000 would be enough to control the stock, then selling near 20. Jacob Little caught the scent of a bear hunt and the game was on. The "Morrison" was bulled to 185 by 1835, and the shorts were caught. They escaped in precedent-setting fashion, by running to the exchange authorities to get the contracts declared void.

The "Morrison" fell on hard times with the advent of railroads, losing money directly and through its banking activity. The speculators lost interest, what with the railroads' better prospects and variety of investment products. In 1844, the company was reorganized and virtually disappeared from the stock lists. The canal passed to the state in 1922 and was closed in 1924. Mules, barges, tow paths, and waterways are now just a pleasant memory of a bygone era.

PART 3

THE GILDED AGE
(1848–1872)

CHAPTER 23

BULLS AND BEARS (1848)

After gold was discovered at Sutter's Mill near present-day Placerville in California, many sought and some found fortune in the camp called Hangtown, which at that time rivaled San Francisco and included builder Mark Hopkins and meatpacker Phillip Armour as residents.

Among the diversions sought by the miners on a Sunday afternoon was the bullfight that had long been a part of California's development under Mexican rule. The bullfight, which had been introduced to Spain by the Moors in the 11th century, was brought to Mexico by the Spanish and was part of fiesta held regularly at the mission-presidio complexes established between 1536 and 1823. The Mexicans added a wrinkle of their own by arranging fights between the Spanish bulls, first brought to the new world by Columbus, and the native grizzly bear that roamed the California coast.

The Spanish longhorn cattle were brought to Mexico in quantity in 1521 and virtually ran wild until Texas became a state in 1845. The longhorn had a keenly developed sense of survival and often encountered the grizzly in the wild.

The game that entertained the miners was to chain a 1,000-pound grizzly to a huge stake in the middle of an arena and then turn the bull into the same arena. The fights were short and violent with the bull sometimes winning by impaling the bear and tossing him *up* over his shoulder. Mostly the bear won by meeting the charge between the horns and using his enormous paws to wrestle the 1,500-pound bear *down* to the ground, often breaking his neck in the process.

Since the gold discoveries created a flood of trading in mining

FIGURE 23–1
The grizzly bear and the longhorn bull. The bear usually won!

shares, both in San Francisco and New York, the terms *bull* and *bear* were introduced into the investment jargon to describe opponents in setting market direction. The analogy had been used before by the Spanish writer Don José de la Vega in 1688, but the active Civil War markets established the terms for all time.

The first person to be called a bear or bull was Jacob Little, who made his mark by introducing short selling in the panic of 1837. He made and lost four fortunes in the years that preceded the Civil War and was dubbed "The Little Bear" by fellow traders. He escaped a corner in Erie Railroad by buying convertible bonds that had been sold in England, unbeknown to the bulls, and he converted the bonds to cover his short position.

The two combatants that focused the terms for all time were the bear, Daniel Drew, and the bull, Cornelius Vanderbilt. The analogy fit perfectly the gigantic struggles between these two titans that went on for 30 years over steamboats and railroads.

Vanderbilt was as straightforward and optimistic as a bull, while Drew was devious, without scruples, and always trying to wrestle the market lower. These two bumped heads continually with a fight over the Harlem Railroad, during the Civil War, producing a typical encounter.

Vanderbilt had been accumulating shares of the road for a number of years and introduced improvements to the line. Uncle Daniel was attracted when the stock started to move and joined in the buying to give the price an artificial boost from $8 to $100. He then cooperated with the politician "Boss" Tweed to mount a massive bear attack on the road. They went heavily short of the stock, and Tweed used his influence to get the Harlem's right-of-way rescinded.

Vanderbilt let them "operate" until the stock dropped to $72. They had sold 137,000 shares, even though only 110,000 shares were outstanding. Vanderbilt then began soaking up the shares held by others and advanced the price to $179, forcing the bears to terms with the Commodore.

But then Drew attacked again, selling the stock down to $100 before Vanderbilt began to squeeze again. He raised the price to $285 and offered to settle again. Drew, hat in hand, pleaded with the Commodore and was finally excused with a $500,000 loss.

Vanderbilt advised Drew: "After this, never sell what you haven't got, Dannie." Which prompted Dan'l to compose his famous couplet: "He who sells what isn't his'n, must buy it back or go to prison."

In the gold camps, the bear defeated the bull in any fair fight. On Wall Street, the smart money follows the bull. Daniel Drew died broke, unable even to fulfill pledges to his church (he was short there too!), while Commodore Vanderbilt left his son William a fortune of $80 million.

CHAPTER 24

CHICKEN MANIA (1853)

After gold was discovered in California, speculation in American markets accelerated rapidly. The canal and rail systems were supplying the industrial complex with resources and distributing the finished products. For the first time in the nation's history, the cash was flowing. Gold production in California soon became $500 million per year, and mining shares were a basis for speculation in California and New York.

All this activity generated the fuel for wild speculations in stocks, real estate, and commodities. Guano (gull excretions) was one of the popular items. The deposits of hundreds of years by bats, seals, and gulls were collected from the islands off the coast of Peru, and an active market was established to trade the commodity. The practical application was as fertilizer and remained so until the early 20th century when low-cost nitrogen products replaced the use of guano. If it were not for technology, guano futures might be a popular item for the Chicago Board of Trade today. It would give new meaning to the term *a guano spread.*

Not that there needs to be a practical use for the commodity. Witness the tulip craze of 17th-century Holland. Those flowers were just for trading, which is reminiscent of the old joke about three commodity traders who were "into" sardines. The first trader bought a thousand cans of sardines for $6 per can and had soon sold them to the second trader for $7. This trader in turn passed them along to trader three for $8. The last owner opened a can and ate a sardine and began reading the riot act to the seller. "These sardines are no good—they're rancid!" Replied the second trader: "Of course they're no good. Those sardines are not for eating—they're for trading!"

While the gold rush was on in California, chicken mania came to Boston.

Darwin had suggested that the chicken originated with the red jungle fowl of southeast Asia, and evidence points to domestication as early as 3,000 B.C. Captain Cook found it thriving along with the dog and the pig on all the islands he visited (including Hawaii). The Egyptians apparently discovered its use as meat and for eggs. The Romans employed scientific methods to production of both food products. Aristotle and Pliny the Elder had long been considering the eternal question: Which came first, the chicken or the egg?

But these chickens were for eating—they weren't for trading! When the port of Canton was opened in 1834, one of the first trading vessels returned to England with a number of birds, which were called initially *Shanghai* or *Chittagong* and later *cochin,* as a present for the young Queen Victoria. The strange-looking birds created quite a sensation, and the queen's interest heightened the effect. The term *Cochin* described the region now known as Vietnam—specifically the Mekong Delta area—and the birds were melanoid in color, with dark bones, rose combs, and feathered shanks. Everyone wanted a pair for breeding purposes.

The birds were exhibited in Birmingham, England, in 1850, and tens of thousands came to see them, but this was after the mania struck America.

On November 15 and 16 of 1849, Boston held the Grand Show of Domestic Poultry and Convention of Fowl Breeders and Fanciers in the public garden. Over 10,000 spectators inspected 1,023 birds of all breeds and varieties with prizes given. Joining in the praise of the chicken was the great Daniel Webster.

Every year thereafter for over a hundred years, the poultry show was held, and it was copied by a number of other cities. Doctors, lawyers, and ministers led the breeding and showing revolution. The farmers were still eating their investments.

Along with the Cochins came other Asiatic fowl, and combinations with European breeds were tried in infinite permutations. And the price was going up!

Soon the cost of the henhouse was more than the cost of the breeder's cottage. The chickens' shelter had to be kept clean, dry, warm, and secure.

By 1853, the country was in a speculative frenzy. There were hen brokers in Boston, New Orleans, and London. Breeders hired press agents to herald the characteristics of their new breeds. Reminiscent of the tulip mania, prices lost all touch with value and reality. A pair of Cochin Spanish fowl sold for $700. Gray Chittagongs sold for $50 each. Shanghais were priced at $100. One man in Boston sold $23,000 worth of "fancy" poultry in 1853.

But like all manias, the bubble burst. Prices for the birds dropped precipitously, and interest passed back from professional men turned amateur breeders to the professional farmers interested in meat and egg production.

One of the leading breeders of that day found that his prize Shanghai cock was no longer salable, killed it, cooked it, and ate it for dinner. To make matters worse, it turned out to be a very tough bird.

CHAPTER 25

THE FIRST BEAR ON WALL STREET (1857)

In 1678, Charles Wooley, a graduate of Cambridge, visited New York and described the city as "poore, scanty in population, its buildings mostly of wood, some few of stone and wood."

Fortunately for those of us interested in history, Mr. Wooley went on to record the first bear hunt held on Wall Street. Actually, it took place on Pearl Street, just north of Wall Street and the wall in 1678. Mr. Wooley calls the play by play: "In an orchard of Mr. John Robinson of New York, where we followed a bear from tree to tree, upon which he would swarm like a cat; and when he got his resting place upon a high branch, we dispatched a youth after him with a club to an opposite bough who, knocking his claws, he comes tumbling down backwards with a thump upon the ground, so we after him again."

Many other bears (and bulls) of the two-legged variety were to prowl the streets in the following three centuries, and the parade hasn't ended yet.

The terms *bear* and *bull* applied to stock market participants originated in gold rush days and the label of *bear* was first applied to Jacob Little, the first successful stock speculator in the United States and the man credited with introducing the concept of short selling.

Jacob Little received his early financial education as a clerk in Jacob Barker's employ. Barker was a well-to-do merchant who also brokered stocks. Commodity trading was the big thing at that time, with a limited list of securities and little public interest in trading shares. Jacob Little was one of the first and certainly the first of any success and note.

In 1835, Jacob Little founded a brokerage firm with his brother and accumulated a fortune in the panic and crash of 1837. Barker went bankrupt during the depression.

The panic of 1837 was induced by President Jackson's hard money policies. This led to a reduction of land speculation in the West, bringing on contraction, panic, depression, and bank failures—all in all, a good environment for Little's predilection for short selling.

The panic soured investors on repudiated state bonds, and in 1838, a variety of railroad shares were first offered to a public ready for a change in investments and more attuned to speculation. By 1840, there was a market in American shares in London, and eventually Erie bonds, convertible into stock, were bought and sold there.

Little started a bear campaign on Erie common shares, disposing of large blocks on sellers options, which allowed 6 to 12 months for delivery of the certificates. A clique of bulls decided to corner him by absorbing the floating supply and forcing Little to terms.

Some of the members of the "corner" were Erie directors, certain that they could account for all shares of the railroad. Long forgotten were the convertible bonds sold to London earlier.

On the day when delivery was required, Little appeared at the offices of the Erie with his bonds in hand, quietly invoked the convertibility privilege and, satisfied his sellers option contracts. This broke the market and let Little escape to play another day.

His successful escape was much imitated in days to come— particularly by Drew, Gould, and Fisk in escaping a corner engineered by Commodore Vanderbilt in the same Erie stock. Little's maneuver resulted in a change in the New York Stock Exchange rules limiting the duration of sellers options to 60 days.

Jacob Little went on to gain and lose four fortunes in a 20-year Wall Street career, finally going down for the count in the panic of 1857. Ironically, he was still on the short side of the market, but unfortunate enough to be extended going into the last rally before the 1857 crash. Too soon is too bad on the short side. Little was short 100,000 shares of Erie and failed for $10 million on December 5, 1856, in a period of rising prices, just before the precipitous drop. Erie sold for 63 ⅞ in January 1857 and as low as 8 in October of the same year.

Little loved the game and bemoaned the hours when the exchanges were closed. He was always campaigning for longer hours, even while frequenting an evening exchange that operated uptown, away from the financial district.

After his fourth failure, he was still wandering about the Street, trying to raise the capital to enter the game once more. A true market leader until the end, his last words were: "I am going up—who will go with me?"

CHAPTER 26

THE COMMODORE'S CORNERS (1863)

Cornelius Vanderbilt was born while George Washington was president. During the War of 1812, Vanderbilt transported supplies for the U.S. army. His conveyor was a sailboat bought with money earned from plowing his father's farm. With his army earnings, he built a schooner and was soon running a ferry service between Staten Island and Manhattan.

After the steamboat had been perfected, Cornelius started providing transportation on the Hudson, between New York and Albany. His ships were fast and profitable, and he soon attracted Daniel Drew as competition.

Drew started as a drover and then was the proprietor of the Bullshead Tavern, where he invested in a friend's steamboat. When Vanderbilt (a commodore by now) drove the friend out of business, Drew took up the challenge. Eventually an alliance was arranged and both prospered.

In 1845, the *New York Sun* ran a list of property owners in New York worth $100,000 or more. Vanderbilt was listed at $250,000, Drew $300,000, and Jacob Little, a leading Wall Street broker, was worth $500,000. The big money was in the real estate of the Astors, Van Renaselaers, and Whitneys.

When gold was discovered in California, Drew went to Wall Street to speculate, while Vanderbilt went to Nicaragua to build a transportation system across the isthmus. Drew was to spend the remainder of his life as a speculator and to die destitute after reaching a pinnacle of $13 million. Vanderbilt spent his life building and died with $80 million in hand.

Transporting men and supplies to the gold fields across

FIGURE 26–1
Commodore Cornelius Vanderbilt

Courtesy of Brown Brothers Stock Photos

Nicaragua built the Commodore's fortune. He used boats and stagecoaches, fought the heat and the plague, and worked 16-hour days. In the 1850s, he had over 100 ships afloat and earned $100,000 per month. By 1853, his net worth was estimated to be $11 million.

The Commodore was as tough as nails and was never known to back down from any fight, as later events were to prove. He once had a piece of property seized by associates while he was on a European vacation, so he wrote them from Europe:

Gentlemen:

You have undertaken to cheat me. I will not sue you, for law takes too long. I will ruin you.

Sincerely yours

Cornelius Van Derbilt

and he was as good as his word.

Vanderbilt and Drew entered the directorate of the New York and Harlem Railroad (Harlem) together in 1857. Drew was already active in the Erie. The two men had fought and collaborated over steamships for over 20 years and were now about to spend a decade doing the same thing with railroads.

The Commodore went at the Harlem as he attacked any other problem. He bought shares and replaced management and added improvements. Harlem stock selling for $6 in October 1857 was at 28 by January 1863 when Vanderbilt assumed control. The stage was set for the two most famous stock corners in market history. In the first, the Common Council of the City of New York found itself cornered, and the second trapped the New York Legislature.

The Commodore wanted to operate a streetcar line along Broadway, from 42nd Street to the Battery. So he approached the politician "Boss" Tweed and made the liberal payments of stock and cash required to secure the support of the New York Common Council. The price of the Harlem began to rise.

Now Drew approached Tweed and suggested that they short the Harlem in partnership with the aldermen and then repeal the Commodore's franchise. Harlem now was at 75.

The council filled its short positions, and the Commodore began laying rails and absorbing all the stock offered. The council repealed the francise, and the judge in the court of common appeals issued an injunction prohibiting the laying of rails on Broadway. The stock dropped—but only three points—as the Harlem was cornered.

With the shorts panicked, the price rose to 179. The city council hastily repealed the repeal, and Vanderbilt let the aldermen off for a million-dollar loss. Drew and the remaining shorts restocked Vanderbilt's petty cash with another $4 million.

Now Vanderbilt went to Albany with his "grease" to get legislation allowing the merger of his Hudson and Harlem Railroads. The legislature was willing, and the governor promised to sign the bill. The stock had settled back below 90 after the corner was broken, but began to rise again and was around 150 in early 1864.

The legislators pocketed the Commodore's bribe, shorted the stock as a group, considered the legislation, and defeated the bill. Drew had joined the fray as their leader.

Harlem shares dropped to 90 quickly, but the legislators decided that 50 would be a good place to cover. The Commodore had a serious battle on his hands. This time he needed help, and he soon had an alliance with John Tobin and Leonard Jerome. They were soon accepting all Harlem and Hudson stock being offered. It wasn't long until they had accepted 27,000 shares more than existed! That is to say, the bears had guaranteed to deliver shares that didn't exist anywhere except in Vanderbilt's safe. The Harlem was cornered again.

By June, the price of Harlem stock was at 285, and the Commodore was definitely in command, with the bears on their knees. A compromise was proposed to him and he replied: "Put it up to 1,000. This panel game is being tried too often."

Vanderbilt's partners started to reason with the Commodore, Jerome pointing out that his threat "would break every house on the Street." Vanderbilt agreed to settle for the 285 figure, and Drew and the legislators were off the hook again, but with heavy losses. In one day, 15,000 shares settled at the 285 figure. The great bear, Drew, slunk away to lick his wounds, and a score of the honorable members of the legislature had to leave Albany without paying their board bills.

CHAPTER 27

SCARLET LADY OF WALL STREET (1868)

"Two streaks of rust," is the way the line's own engineers described the New York and Lake Erie Railroad (Erie). The "scarlet lady" was the label Wall Street appended, as Jacob Little, Daniel Drew, Cornelius Vanderbilt, Jay Gould, Jim Fisk, and William Trevor all sought her favors.

The Erie railroad was chartered in 1832 to connect ocean traffic at New York City with the Great Lakes. Local politicians, envious of the Erie Canal, had forced the railroad over a mountainous route that was hard to maintain and away from the rich markets of Pennsylvania. It took nearly 20 years to complete, with several bankruptcies enroute, and it never reached its intended terminals of Buffalo and New York City.

By 1836, the road had been built about halfway to the lakes when the company ran out of money. The New York legislature wouldn't supply more, but English investors—fascinated by railroads—bought the Erie bonds and saw the road continued.

The euphoria attending the additional funding carried over to the stock market, and when the panic of 1837 came along, the Erie was particularly vulnerable. Jacob Little got his start as the market's first great speculator by selling Erie stock contracts for future delivery, and when the bulls tried to trap him by cornering Erie, Little responded by sending to England for convertible bonds. In the panic, prices fell heavily and Little was established. However, just before the panic of 1857, Little was again short of Erie and because he was early the "lady" did him in.

When the road was completed in 1851 (short of the two terminals), it was in poor shape and travel upon it was questionable. Thirty serious accidents occurred in 1852 alone. And as always, the line was strapped for capital.

About this time, Daniel Drew started circling the Erie much as a vulture would a wounded prey. Daniel bought some shares and offered the line better rates with his trunk lines in western New York. This gambit won him a seat on the directors, and by 1854, he was treasurer of the line. For the next 12 years, he worked the Erie like a virtuoso, making the stock move up and down at his will.

In 1859, Vanderbilt started buying stock and became a director. Vanderbilt was a builder, and he wanted to complete a line between New York and Chicago. The line had gone into receivership after the 1857 panic and was reorganized as the Erie Railway with some stability under a new president. The Erie prospered until 1864, when the president, Nathaniel Marsh, died. The "speculative director" (Drew) was in charge again and by lending money and starting rumors was manipulating the stock.

The third actor in the melodrama enters in the personage of John Eldridge, a Boston banker, representing the Boston Hartford and Erie railroad and wanting the Erie to finance a connection with its line to New England. The scramble for stock and control was on.

Drew formed an alliance with Eldridge against Vanderbilt, but soon found himself odd man out as Vanderbilt and Eldridge reached an agreement.

Drew went to Vanderbilt, as he had been doing for years under stress, begged his forgiveness, and asked to be retained as a director. Eldridge was now president, Drew retained treasurer, and two new directors appointed were James Fisk and Jay Gould.

Now all the actors were on stage and the props were ready. These consisted of: a printing press, suitcases, a rowboat, and a Jersey City hotel, dubbed Fort Taylor.

Vanderbilt soon found that he wasn't in control of the line and set out to change that. He started buying the floating supply of the common while laying the groundwork to prevent increasing the capitalization.

A provision of the General Railroad Act of 1850 prohibited rail companies from increasing their stock, but allowed convertible bonds. Drew allied himself with Gould and Fisk, and they held the majority vote of the executive committee, authorizing $5 million in bonds for improvements on the road. The bonds were issued, sold, and converted, and the stock thrown on the market. Vanderbilt absorbed this "water" plus the short sales by Drew, Gould, and Fisk.

The tricky trio did it again, and Vanderbilt finally caught on when he began absorbing fresh certificates with Jim Fisk's name on them. "If this damned printing press doesn't break down, we'll give the old hog all he wants of Erie," was Fisk's war cry.

Vanderbilt sent the law for them; Drew packed $7 million in greenbacks in suitcases and headed out of Vanderbilt's jurisdiction to New Jersey. Gould and Fisk were dining leisurely at Delmonico's when informed that they were about to be served, so they spent a foggy night in a rowboat crossing the Hudson to Jersey City. The next week was spent barricaded in Fort Taylor with armed guards.

The issue now became a right of the Erie to issue stock, and a battle for legislative votes was imminent as both Gould and Vanderbilt showed up in Albany with bribe money. Gould had to have the legislators call on him because the New York City warrants had been served and his residence was the Albany pokey. Gould passed out thousand-dollar bills with both hands, and he and Vanderbilt soon had distributed some $700,000 between them. Vanderbilt's messenger brought in fresh cash, and Gould intercepted him with a bribe of $70,000 just to disappear.

The Commodore soon became disgusted with the process and pulled out, leaving the legislators bereft and enraged. Almost en masse, the legislators rushed to Gould offering their votes for $100 each, but Gould had snapped shut his valise.

In the meantime, Drew was making his own deal with Vanderbilt, escaping with most of his profit. Vanderbilt got half of his money back, Eldridge got money for the Boston, Hartford, and Erie, and Gould and Fisk got the Erie's empty till. Vanderbilt stated that he had learned "to never kick a skunk."

Drew was out and said, "There ain't nothing left in 'ary," but Gould and Fisk soon proved him wrong. Gould was president and Fisk was managing director. "Boss" Tweed was added to the Erie board.

Fisk started the presses again and $21 million more in stock went on the market. Gould and Fisk went short and caught the outsider, Drew, in their trap. The dynamic duo reversed course and used their short gains to drive the Erie price back up, finishing Drew. Drew tried to have them ousted, but Tweed's connections prevented that.

After some sidetrips into railroad acquisitions and gold speculation, Fisk ran a series of sideshows ending with his death in 1872. Gould was now in trouble as the English shareholders engaged General Daniel Sickles to depose Gould. Sickles marched in with a small army of generals and they set up as directors in a room of the Erie offices. Gould summoned the police, but they were cowed by the roomful of Union army officers. Included in the group was General George B. McClellan, former commander of the army of the Potomac and presidential candidate.

Three days later, Sickles suggested to Gould that he resign, slyly adding: "If you do, Erie will go up 15 points—you can make a million." Gould resigned. The stock went up 20 points, and Gould did make his million.

The new board attempted to recover Gould's plunderings through the courts, and out of court he offered a piece of real estate that he solemnly swore was worth $6 million. Ecstatic to have any success at all with Gould, the board dropped the criminal charges and civil suits. Two years later, it was discovered that the property was really worth only $200,000.

During Gould's six-year tenure, the Erie had been bloated with $64 million in watered stock, requiring 69 years to pass before a dividend could be paid to the shareholders. Gould was 36 in 1872 when he released control and $22 million richer than when he assumed it—and he was just getting started!

CHAPTER 28

JUBILEE JIM (1868)

Jim Fisk failed as a peddler, businessman, broker, operator, and lover, but succeeded gloriously as a showman.

Jim started his career with the circus when he ran away from home because his father made him clean the stables. He traded horses for elephants, applying his basic talents to increased responsibility.

This experience convinced him there were better things in life, and he next took over his father's tin-peddler business. Jim added some show biz with four white horses, shining brass, and a stovepipe hat. He bought his supplies from Boston and soon became an agent for his supplier, selling to the army in Washington during the Civil War. The combination of letters to influential men and his contacts with disreputable women led to the lucrative sale of deficient blankets to the government. "You can sell the government anything," he gloated.

Jim soon set himself up in contraband sales. He personally bought cotton in the Confederate South at 12 cents per pound and then ran the cotton through Union lines to the New England mills, where he sold it for $2 per pound. Had the war lasted longer, he would have been set for life.

The war did end—much to his chagrin—but he took one last profit out of the English by having a fast boat chartered at Halifax, Virginia, and when Lee surrendered, Fisk's agents sailed for England, where they sold $5 million in Confederate bonds on the London Exchange, five days before word of the Confederacy's fall reached there.

Armed with $60,000, Fisk went into the dry-goods business. This soon failed, and he migrated to Wall Street with the remnants of his stake to try speculation.

FIGURE 28–1
Jim Fisk

Courtesy of Brown Brothers Stock Photos

His career as a speculator ended quickly when his funds disappeared, and he appeared on Daniel Drew's doorstep, offering his services as a broker.

Drew controlled a small Connecticut railroad, the Stovington, and Fisk offered to sell it to some Boston capitalists of his acquaintance at a substantial profit. He did such an outstanding job that Drew was soon using him as front man on a number of jobs. His skill at negotiation was the key.

Fisk was shrewd, bold, and a good-natured, likable fellow, and Drew started tutoring him along with Jay Gould. Drew played Fagin to Fisk and Gould—the artful dodgers—and the pair were quick studies, as Drew was to find out later, much to his displeasure.

Fisk was colorful with his full figure, handlebar mustache, and diamond-studded fingers. He loved to wear a uniform and be the center of attention. With some of his first stock market gains, he started the Narragansett Steamship Company and appointed himself admiral: "If Vanderbilt's a commodore, I guess I should rank as an admiral!"

Each sailing day, Admiral Fisk would appear in full uniform with his mistress, Josie Mansfield, at his side, take up his position on the bridge until the steamer had rounded the tip of Manhattan (out of sight) where a tug was waiting to take him to shore.

William Travers, the noted Wall Street broker, speculator, and wit, visited Fisk on his boat one day and was taken for a tour. Fisk had large portraits of himself and Jay Gould hung at either side of the stairs leading to the saloon cabin.

Fisk pointed out the paintings to Travers and asked if he didn't think they were good. Travers agreed: "I think they are very good—but to make them complete, there should be a picture of our Saviour in the middle!"

After Fisk and Gould ousted Drew from the leadership of the Erie, Gould became president and Fisk vice president. He was then known as the Prince of Erie. Josie became his assistant and was paid $1,000 per month for her services. Always with a mind toward style, Fisk moved the offices of the Erie to Pikes Grand Opera Palace. The offices were located upstairs at the head of a grand staircase leading from an ornate theater lobby. Here Fisk could launch operettas or manipulate the market at will. Gould and Fisk purchased the building in their own names with Erie funds and then leased the building back to the railroad, producing a substantial income for themselves.

Fisk used the offices of the Erie to bestow favors, including supplying the Ninth Army Regiment, which was always strapped for financial reinforcements. For one that had worked hard at avoiding the Civil War, Fisk certainly was patriotic.

The Ninth showed its appreciation by bestowing a uniform and the rank of colonel on Fisk, who was happy to add it to his other titles of admiral and prince.

Fisk would march at the head of the regiment, with flags flying and bands playing. But the militia was called out to put down the Irish (Orangemen) riots. The fighting Irish routed the parading militia, chasing Fisk over back fences with his gold braid flying.

When Jim wasn't playing admiral or colonel or executing one of Gould's devious schemes, he liked to drive his coach and six horses through Central Park, with Josie beside him, on his way to Harlem Lane, where he lost thousands on the horse races. Occasionally,he would replace Josie with a couple of his musical stars. On these occasions, Josie was replacing him with the dandy Ned Stokes. Soon the young lovers were blackmailing Fisk with letters he had written Josie. After being cuckolded for some time, he stopped payment and Josie brought suit.

While the public licked its chops in anticipation of Fisk's and Gould's crimes being exposed, Fisk was ousted from the management of the Erie and on the way to see friends was ambushed and shot by Stokes. Jim Jubilee Fisk, Jr., died as he had lived, sensational to the end.

Stokes spent four years at Sing Sing and was operating a restaurant when he died in 1901. Josie married a wealthy lawyer, who died in an insane asylum. She lived comfortably in Paris until her death in 1931 at age 90.

CHAPTER 29

JAY GOULD'S GOLD (1869)

When the Civil War burst upon the country, the opportunities for wealth quickly multiplied. Commodore Vanderbilt raised some of his sunken steamboats, painted the rotten timbers, and sold them to the war department. J. P. Morgan bought 5,000 defective carbines, which had once been rejected by inspectors, for $3.50 each and sold them to the army in St. Louis for $22 each. The whole lot had to be condemned when men began losing thumbs with the weapons. Morgan kept the money. Jim Fisk sold poor quality army blankets at exorbitant prices to Washington. Lots of opportunity—as articulately expressed by Daniel Drew: "Along with ordinary happenings, we fellows in Wall Street now have, in addition, the fortunes of war to speculate about and that always makes great doings on a stock exchange. It's good fishing in troubled waters."

But the great new game brought to the casinos of Wall Street was the chance to speculate on the price of gold—or more accurately, the price of the greenback, as gold is stable in value and the greenback was not convertible to gold. The paper value changed with every battle.

Trading in gold first started on the floor of the New York Stock Exchange in 1861. The governors soon decided it was unpatriotic to trade gold and, having plenty of stock activity, abolished gold trading. Gold then moved into the open air and began trading on the curb market on William Street.

By 1862, gold activity warranted its own market, and it moved into dismal quarters known as the coal hole.

In October 1864, the New York Gold Exchange was formed and soon moved into new quarters called the Gold Room. Member-

FIGURE 29–1
Jay Gould

Courtesy of Brown Brothers Stock Photos

ship was $25, and interest ran high. A journalist of the time described it thusly: "Imagine a rat-pit in full blast, with 20 or 30 men ringed around the rat tragedy, each with a canine under his arm, yelling and howling at once."

Vanderbilt, Drew, and Gould were busy with railroad speculation, which also was in a frenzy, and the fishing was good, but by 1869, Gould had the Erie under control and with the Civil War over, gold had settled into a narrow trading range of 2 percent.

Gould was seeking to expand his rail empire west and was being thwarted at every turn. He needed money to finance this expansion, so he set out to manipulate the gold market. Whether he intended to corner the market is questionable, but he certainly meant to raise the price of gold.

The amount of gold in the United States was about $100 million at that time, with $20 million in the floating supply. The remainder was held in the U.S. Treasury, and sale was at the discretion of the president. The president who had just taken office was Ulysses S. Grant.

Margin requirements were extremely easy at that time, and Gould decided $100,000 could control the $20 million, provided the government didn't release any of its hoard. To assure that, Gould needed to enact the time-honored principle of fixing the politicians, or at least have an inside information source. Gould was acquainted with Grant's brother-in-law, Abel R. Corbin, whose checkered career included speculation. Corbin quickly promised an introduction to the president, and a meeting took place on Fisk's steamboat when Grant was on his way to Boston. The meeting was frustrating to Gould because the president wasn't clear on what he would do if the gold price rose. Gould went to his fallback option of inside information.

Corbin recommended General Butterfield as the New York assistant treasurer, an open position responsible for gold sales in New York. He was appointed, and Gould soon offered him a $10,000 personal loan. Gould offered to buy $1.5 million of gold in Corbin's name, and the game was on. Gould, whose name had been changed from Gold by his grandfather, was returning to his roots and taking gold off the market.

The price was around $135 in greenbacks when the operation began in early September 1869. By September 22, Fisk was personally leading the charge in the Gold Room, and the price closed at 141 ½. That evening, Gould made his regular visit to Corbin, who had just received a letter from Grant, stating his distress at the gold speculation and implying that he would be releasing bullion from the Treasury.

Gould was caught. He had set Fisk and his brokers in motion on the bull side, but they wouldn't be able to absorb the new supply or the panic that it would induce. Gould quietly approached his old partner and broker Ben Smith and instructed him to sell gold in his behalf. At the close Thursday, the price was 143 ¼, and everyone but Gould expected a continued rise. Fisk and his clique held $110 million in calls for gold. Smith was carefully feeding sell orders through a variety of brokers not connected to Gould. The next day was to be the most eventful in the history of Wall Street and known forever as "Black Friday."

Money was as scarce as gold, and rates were now running ½ percent per day. Everybody was involved in buying, selling, or lending. There were an estimated 15,000 people short of gold, led by Jay Cooke, who had financed the Civil War for the Union. To supply the money for this battle, stocks had been sold mercilessly, with the more speculative issues off 10 percent.

Early on Friday, the streets were thronged, and trades were being made by those unwilling to wait for the 10 o'clock opening. After the opening, the price quickly went to 145 with Fisk ordering his brokers to "put it up to 150." Fisk was soon on the floor calling for 160. Gould sat quietly in a corner of his office shredding newspapers into confetti. Gold went to 165. At 12:07 P.M., it was announced that the government would sell gold, and the great corner broke to 140 immediately. Within 15 minutes the price was back to 133, where it had began a couple of weeks earlier.

The battle had ended, but now everyone had to carry out his own corpse, as Fisk put it. Gould was so haggard that Fisk described him as "Nothing left but a heap of clothes and a pair of eyes."

The mess was enormous. The Gold Exchange Bank went into receivership, and the gold exchange shut down. A number of brokers failed, and one shot himself. Fisk repudiated his contracts, and the lawyers swept in like piranha at feeding time.

Gould eventually extricated his buddy Fisk by having two of "Boss" Tweed's judges issue injunctions restraining collections, and the suits lingered in the courts for six years after Fisk's death.

Ben Smith, Gould's partner who had been used and ruined in Gould's escape, caught up with Gould in the street sometime later and told him: "I'll live to see the day, sir, when you have to earn your living by going around the street with a hand organ and a monkey."

Gould replied: "Maybe you will, Henry, maybe you will. And when I want a monkey, Henry, I'll send for you."

CHAPTER 30

HIS TOUCH WAS DEATH (1869)

"For Vanderbilt and company, 'tis indeed a gilded age
But poverty increases, 'tis thus that tramps are made
Shall it be continued when the peoples votes are weighed
    As we go marching on?
No! We'll hang Jay Gould on a sour apple tree
And bring grief to the plotters of a base monopoly
From the ghouls of booty we shall go free
    As we go marching on."

Antimonopoly song of the 1880s

Jay Gould was undoubtedly the most hated man in Wall Street history. He used and then ran roughshod over everyone of his acquaintance. Jim Fisk was a notable exception to this, but Jim was entertaining, posed no financial threat, and had no qualms about doing Jay's dirty work. All other notable Wall Street financiers in the postbellum period felt the sting of Jay's operations.

Gould had studied under Daniel Drew just after the Civil War and was his partner in the watering of Erie stock, sold to Vanderbilt in 1866. After that episode, Gould considered his education complete and had Drew ousted from the Erie management.

In August 1869, Gould began to manipulate Erie stock, and Drew, no longer the insider, smelled the familiar bear scent. He was soon short of 70,000 shares at 40 per share. Suddenly, the price advanced to 52 ½ in one day and 61 the next. The bear trap had been sprung and had Drew firmly by the leg.

Daniel Drew had been in the short squeeze before with

Vanderbilt, and past strategy called for visiting his opponent and pleading for mercy. It always worked with Vanderbilt. Fisk and Gould were entertained, but unmoved. Drew was cornered, and in November, he was forced to settle at 57 for the stocks sold at 40. Drew was never again a force in Wall Street and issued an appraisal of Gould that was to be repeated often in the next 20 years: "His touch is death!" Shortly after Drew was eliminated as a competitor, Gould sought to make the Erie a more viable railroad by dropping freight rates. A number of trunk lines were fighting for the available business, including Commodore Vanderbilt's New York Central line. These two giants bumped heads over the Buffalo to New York City traffic.

Vanderbilt had made his early wealth in steamboat transportation and had immense success in destroying competition by reducing rates and forcing the smaller lines out of business. The stage was now set for a revival of this tactic.

The point of contention revolved around cattle shipment to New York City. The usual rate was $125 per carload, and Vanderbilt dropped his rate to $100. Gould went to $75. Vanderbilt moved to $50 and Gould countered to $25.

Vanderbilt had enough. He set the livestock rate at $1 per carload and sat back to await the inevitable. Sure enough, the New York Central filled up with cattle while the Erie ran empty. Vanderbilt cackled with glee until he found out several months later that Fisk had bought every steer in Buffalo and shipped them to New York City via the Central.

Vanderbilt was livid with rage as he pondered the truth of Drew's earlier statement. In 1872, he published a notice declaring he would have nothing more to do with Gould "unless it be to defend myself."

Jay Gould was a small man, hidden by a tremendous black beard. His office after 1882 was in the Western Union Building on Broadway. He held controlling interest in the company, and he and Russell Sage were directors.

Gould would be seen slinking along the hallways close to the wall, like an alleycat that expects to be kicked in passing. The corridor door that had his name on it opened into an empty closet. This must have surprised any number of would-be assassins when they thought they were on the threshold of revenge.

The only way to reach Gould was through the Missouri Pacific transfer office, which had a four-foot counter and a bullpen full of palace guards, not to mention Gould's ever-present bodyguard, Giovanni P. Morosini. When callers asked for Jay, an office boy gave them a randomly selected report on his whereabouts. "He's out of town . . . he's at a director's meeting . . . etc."

Cranks and assassination threats were a constant in Gould's life by 1881. In October of that year, he received a letter through the mail signed "victim" that suggested he make his peace with God. Gould offered financial assistance to "victim" through a series of personal column advertisements, while police watched the post office where "victim" continued to mail his correspondence. On November 13, "victim" was caught and turned out to be a ruined speculator who claimed he was only trying to get some "stock tips."

Still, Gould was a constant target for troubled investors. Once Russell Sage had to hide him under a boat on Long Island, carrying food to him for three days. Sage was Gould's last partner and was shrewd and powerful in his own right, always holding the upper hand, managing Gould as Gould had always managed others.

In 1878, Gould had been trapped by a bull clique headed by James R. Keene. Jay was short of Union Pacific stock (his company, of course), and the pool called for settlement of his contracts. On the day appointed for Gould to cover his position, Uncle Russell appeared with a check for $2 million in his pocket, and Gould was saved. However, he paid the price. The remainder of his life, he operated his vast rail and communications empire with Sage pulling the strings in the background.

After another bankruptcy scare in the panic of 1884, Gould died with his fortune intact—some $80 million, but short of Sage's more quiet accumulation and far short of the leading industrialists of the day—Carnegie and Rockefeller, notably. For someone that was so dominant in Wall Street for 25 years, very little remains to remind us that he was even there.

CHAPTER 31

WHERE ARE THE CUSTOMERS' YACHTS? (1870)

William Travers gave up a grocery business in Baltimore and moved to Wall Street, where he became a partner of Leonard Jerome, who in turn became the maternal grandfather of Winston Churchill.

Travers stuttered and took quite a ribbing over it, although he gave as well as he got. When an acquaintance from Baltimore visited him on the Street, it was noted that his stutter was worse in New York City. "W-h-y, y-e-s," replied Travers: "Of course it is. This is a d-d-damned sight b-b-bigger city."

Another time Travers visited a pet shop and was trying to find out if a parrot could talk. After stuttering out the words, the owner quickly replied: "If it couldn't talk better than you, I'd cut its damn head off!"

Travers came into possession of a small yacht in lieu of a debt, and he was sailing at Newport one day when told there was to be a race. Soon a squadron of yachts appeared, and Travers saw that the owners were all bankers and brokers of his acquaintance. When they had assembled on Travers's deck, he was seen scanning the horizon for each new boat and told each time that it belonged to another broker. Finally Travers asked his distinguished visitors: "Wh-wh-where are the cu-cu-customers' yachts?"

Travers once told a friend to come to him in September, and he would give him a point. A point was a stock market tip, as eagerly sought then as today. When the friend appeared, Travers said: "Come for that point? Well you're a lucky dog as I played that point and lost a lot of money. You stay with me and you'll end up in the poorhouse."

A similar story is told of two market speculators who never seemed to make any money and who began to badger a plunger with a big reputation to give them a point. After ignoring them as long as he could, the plunger finally recommended a stock and they rushed off to buy it. The stock soon dropped, creating a significant loss for the pair, so they sought out the tip-giver to furnish him with a piece of their minds. Just as they were approaching their adviser, one of them had second thoughts, telling his partner: "Maybe we shouldn't complain—he might not give us any more points!"

Travers liked to follow the ponies, and he ran into a plunger by the name of Walton at Saratoga Racetrack. Walton told Travers that he had made $350,000 on horse racing in two years. Walton proposed exchanging points with Travers. Travers response was: "I'll give you a first-rate point. If you've made that much in two years—then stick to your business."

Travers entered Wall Street just before the Civil War and started his career on the right side of the 1857 panic and depression. He opened a brokerage firm with Jerome in 1863 and spent the remainder of his career as a broker and social leader.

Cornelius Vanderbilt became a customer of Jerome and Travers and allowed them to join him in his cornering of the Harlem and Hudson Railroads. Jerome was a clever floor trader, and Travers was in demand for social events. Both were smart enough to recognize their limits and the power of their clients, so they had long and profitable Wall Street careers. Travers served the same function with Vanderbilt that Keene was to accomplish with Morgan later.

Another broker of note late in the 19th century was Edward Harriman. Like so many others, he got his start as a quotation boy (known as a pad-shover) and was able to study the operations of Vanderbilt, Gould, and Keene. In 1869, while still a brokerage office clerk, he sold Jay Gould's gold corner short and secured his first $3,000 stake. He used this to buy an exchange seat and open his own office. He soon became known as a gifted technician and expert in railroad stocks. In 1881, he became a director of the Illinois Central Railroad and soon had controlling interest. He then became interested in the proposed reorganization of the much larger Union Pacific. A major battle for control of the Northern

Pacific with Union Pacific pitted against J. P. Morgan eventually developed into one of Wall Street's classic corners.

Another broker spent 50 years in Wall Street and wrote a principal history by that title. He was Henry Clews. Clews came to the Street at the same time as Travers and was a great admirer of his wit. Besides documenting the activity of 50 years, Clews was also the first discount broker. In order to establish himself as a broker, he offered to trade for one sixteenth of a point commission, which was half of the fixed rate at that time. His firm became a fixture on Broad Street, occupying a good portion of the Mills Building, across from the New York Stock Exchange entrance on Broad Street.

Clews was bald, pompous, and the ready object of Travers's wit. Clews tells of entering the Union Club one day after he had been featured in the newspaper as an up-and-coming young businessman.

Travers was sitting with a group of brokers and bankers and when Clews entered, Travers said: "Hallo, boys! Here comes Clews—the self-made man!" Then addressing Clews directly, he said: "I s-s-say, Cl-Cl-Clews, as you are a s-self-made man, wh-wh-why the d-d-devil didn't you put more h-h-hair on the top of your head?"

CHAPTER 32

THE SILVER FOX (1872)

Most of us are investors. We look for some growth in capital along with a fixed return from a more or less stable principal. We are risk-averse. By contrast, a speculator seeks huge profits and assumes the corresponding risk. The speculator plays a fair game and by assuming unpopular positions lends some stability to markets in turmoil. Because maximum risk is encountered when maximum return is sought, few speculators survive long-term involvement in the markets or accumulate much wealth. James R. Keene was such a speculator.

James R. Keene, the silver fox of Wall Street, was the most successful speculator in Wall Street history, starting with little and ending the same way but with spectacular results in between. Others accumulated more money or held it longer, but they were industrialists, manipulators, insiders, or otherwise had some advantage that made success more likely.

Keene was born in England, came to the United States as a youth, and studied law in the South. In 1853, he moved to San Francisco to practice mining law and began sampling some of the penny mining stocks that his clients touted.

Keene worked hard, had a physical breakdown, and was advised by his doctors to take a long sea vacation. After a year's absence and lack of communication with San Francisco, Keene returned to find one of his stocks worth $200,000. He gave up the law, joined the San Francisco exchange, and immediately began to short the various Comstock mining enterprises that were forming a bubble. The results were extraordinary. Keene's $200,000 soon became $4 million. In 1872, Keene departed for Europe—again for his health—but found himself in New York and sampling Wall Street.

Keene's phenomenal timing held as he arrived during a depressed market and soon ran his $4 million into $14 million.

Then his luck changed: First he met Jay Gould and joined him and Major Selover in an attempt to put down Western Union. Gould was a principal of the company and a large shareholder but not at all averse to selling his company short.

Keene and Selover sold the stock in large blocks, but it was absorbed as fast as it was thrown out. It was suspected by the partners that Jay Gould was the culprit.

Selover brooded over his losses, until one day he left the exchange and encountered Gould at the corner of New Street and Exchange Place. Without ceremony, he grabbed the little man by the collar and seat of his pants and dropped him into the entryway of a lower level barbershop.

Gould promptly picked himself up, went quietly to his office, and made a transaction by which Selover lost $15,000 more. After this incident, Gould would always be found in the company of his bodyguard.

It took Gould a little longer to get even with the Silver Fox for encouraging Selover's assault, but Gould's strength was in his patience.

Keene was diversifying his investments and had visions of cornering wheat. He was well on his way when Addison Cammack informed Gould of the operation. The Silver Fox was within a hair's breadth of pulling it off, having control of 25 million bushels, when Gould went short of the market. The price tumbled, brokers called for more margin, banks called in short-term loans, and Keene was technically bankrupt, losing some $7 million in just a few days.

Keene was no longer a threat with his own money, but became J. P. Morgan's adviser and floor broker and benefited by that arrangement. He was, on occasion, able to needle Gould, as an incident in 1881 demonstrates. A spring storm downed the telegraph wires, and Gould had to rely on messengers to place his orders. Keene teamed with Addison Cammack (partners were temporary at best) and William Travers to kidnap Gould's messenger and replace him with one of their own. Travers set up an office across from Gould's townhouse, where he intercepted Gould's orders and acted on them before sending them on their way. The trio nicked Gould pretty good before he caught on to the plot.

After Keene was reduced to brokering, Bernard Baruch became his messenger and protégé. Baruch began as a runner for Arthur Housman in 1891 and started scouting companies for Keene in 1895.

Keene was an ardent turfman. He owned and raced his own horses and backed his judgment with money. Baruch was his bookie, and Keene sent him to the track with thousands in his pockets, and often his clothes bulged with the winnings on the return trip. The future millionaire and adviser to presidents was literally sweating with the responsibility as he rode the ferry back from Coney Island.

Baruch built his credentials with Keene, and he was able to participate in a number of deals that Keene brokered, including the "watered" U.S. Steel Corporation that J. P. Morgan organized. Keene orchestrated the sale of stock to the public, carefully selling while buying some back, creating interest much as a fisherman is known to play a big game fish.

One of Keene's close friends and associate broker was Jacob Field. Field was once asked at a dinner party what he thought of Balzac. Field's reply: "I never deal in dem outside stocks!" Balzac himself had noted earlier: "I do not regard a broker as a member of the human race!"

While he was still in the chips, Keene was once asked why he continued speculating. His reply: "Why does a dog chase his thousandth rabbit? All life is a speculation. The spirit of speculation is born with men."

PART 4

THE MONEY GAME
(1875–1901)

CHAPTER 33

THE SPECIALIST (1875)

In 1875, a Big Board broker named Boyd broke his leg and improved chances for you and me to make money.

After the Civil War, the number of issues traded and volume of transactions increased significantly on the New York Stock Exchange. The method of establishing prices before 1870 was by the *call through*. This involved a roll call of all issues once (twice later) per day, and the bidding process established the price that was honored until the next call through.

While prices were being established by the regular board, pits were in use in the adjacent long room, trading popular stocks in a fashion similar to commodity futures trading today. This transition from auction to continuous trading eventually eliminated the call through by 1871, and trading was by outcry in the pits at the time Boyd broke his leg.

Unable to rush from pit to pit with his orders because of the leg, Boyd took a chair onto the floor of the exchange and announced that he would buy and sell Western Union only. This was one of the popular stocks, and Boyd was soon filling orders for other brokers.

Since brokers had a variety of orders and often missed the best prices as they scurried from point to point, placing limit orders (specific price) with Boyd ensured good execution and justified his fee. This specialization process soon spread to other popular issues and the efficient execution of limit orders began in earnest.

Today each stock traded on the New York Stock Exchange is handled through a specialist. This person is a member of the exchange who receives commissions in addition to trading for his own account. In return, he must agree to make an orderly market by buying to certain limits when the market is falling and selling into demand. In normal times, he can take advantage of minor imbalances for his own profit.

The specialist maintains a "book" with buy orders on one page and sell orders on an adjacent page. He matches orders in his book and his personal account with floor brokers buying or selling at the market.

Most individuals trade "at the market." This means they get the worst end of the bid-ask spread. For instance, the specialist may have orders to buy at 20 ¼ and to sell at 20 ½. The market is somewhere within that range, and if you offer to buy without limit, then you'll get the only price offered for sale, which is 20 ½.

You also introduce the uncertainty created by the delay between being given a quotation and the order reaching the specialist. For these reasons, it is usually to the individual's advantage to set a *limit* on the price he is willing to assume. He thereby eliminates surprise and guarantees good execution (or none at all).

Being able to visualize the specialist's book will improve your results. Human nature influences price choices around important numbers, and this creates a "rebound" effect. Studies have shown that intraday trading does not completely follow random walk as prices cluster around whole numbers, halves, etc., in diminishing frequency. This creates reflecting barriers that the technician would identify as support or resistance.

This effect becomes more pronounced for the higher priced stocks. If you want to sell your IBM above the market of 122 ⅝, you may ask 130 or 125 or even 123, but rarely will you specify 122 ⅞, which is over 10 times more likely to be executed than 123. The specialist will have many entries for 123, and you would go to the bottom of the list. But 122 ⅞ is likely to be blank in his book.

Placing your bids or asked prices away from the market can be done on a probability basis using standard statistical methods to measure and predict variation. The volatility of the stock under consideration and the time you are willing to wait are the principal variables influencing the probability of success.

Today the volatility created by the expiration of options and futures contracts for market indexes has resulted in experimental disclosure of the entries in the specialists' books for the major stocks involved in indexes. This occurs one hour before the close of trading on the last day of the contract period. This reduces the tendency for major traders to panic over unknown or imagined imbalances in buy and sell orders.

In the over-the-counter market, where there are no specialists, part of the book can be displayed on the computer, giving you a feel for the direction of the market in a particular stock. It works very well without the specialist being involved and certainly without human biases that disturb the rhythm of a random walk. It's just a matter of time until the specialist system goes the way of the call through and the computer takes over the job it has been prepped for.

CHAPTER 34

THE GENERAL'S LAST BATTLE (1884)

After General Grant had won a narrow margin of victory at the blood battle of Shiloh, his critics demanded that he be removed from his post. President Lincoln replied: "I can't spare this man—he fights!"

Ulysses S. Grant was a fighter all his life. Although he showed no talent as a youth—except for handling horses—he went to West Point against his will and graduated in the middle of his class. After duty in the Mexican War, he resigned from the army at age 32.

He tried farming and failed. Then it was real estate with the same results. When the Civil War broke out, he was working in his father's leather store, and the governor of Illinois made him a colonel for an unruly outfit. Within a year, he had whipped the unit into shape and was a brigadier general. In March 1864, Lincoln appointed him commander of all Union land forces, and less than five years later he was president of the United States.

Grant served two terms and retired to New York City. His love of horses persisted, and he would race his carriage up and down Harlem Lane. Evenings he spent playing cards with his cronies.

In 1880, his son, U.S., Junior, known as "Buck," met Ferdinand Ward and joined him in a brokerage firm known as Grant and Ward. Ward knew and took advantage of the drawing power of the Grant name.

Ward was a personable young man, originally employed by the Produce Exchange, where he met James D. Fish, president of Marine National Bank. Fish and Ward soon were speculating in Produce Exchange membership certificates. The venture was successful, and Ward resigned his job to join Fish in stock speculation. By the time he met Buck Grant, he had accumulated a small fortune.

Ward, Grant, and Fish each contributed $100,000 to the partnership, Fish being a silent partner. U.S. Grant, Sr., added $50,000 later in the year and became a limited partner. Buck soon had his brother, Jesse, and his father-in-law invested in the firm, so it became a Grant family enterprise.

Ward was an exceptional salesman, and the general's name was used freely with his clients. Outstanding profits were paid— mostly out of fresh money from new investors—as the markets went into decline in 1883.

Henry Clews relates a story in *Fifty Years in Wall Street* demonstrating how click Ferdinand was. Clews knew a man that invested $50,000 with Ward and then went abroad. About six months later, he returned and called on Grant and Ward to check progress on his investment. Ward—known as the Napoleon of finance—looked up his account and wrote him a check for $250,000, less his commission. The man was so overwhelmed by his windfall that he lay awake that night calculating how he might turn the $250,000 into millions.

After breakfast the next day, Clews's friend hustled down to Grant and Ward to redeposit his money. Ward met him with a smile, took his check, gave him a receipt, and within two weeks the firm had folded. The failure of Grant and Ward and the Marine National Bank precipitated the panic of 1884. Just before the failure, Fish had lent most of the bank's resources to try to prop up Ward's firm. At the last moment, Ward approached General Grant about a loan to shore up the Marine Bank. Grant was shocked at the situation, and Buck was surprised too.

Grant had no money, but went to William H. Vanderbilt, the Commodore's son and an old friend. Vanderbilt told him he cared not a whit for the Marine National or Grant and Ward, but he would lend the ex-president the money on his word alone.

When Grant delivered the check to Ferdinand Ward, Ward cashed it and disappeared. The brokerage firm was bankrupt, and the Marine National closed its doors. Fish went to jail, and Grant was in debt and stuck with the stigma of the whole affair.

Grant called on Vanderbilt and insisted on signing over all his assets, including war trophies, which were refused. A compromise was finally struck with the trophies being given to the Smithsonian.

Searching for a way to rehabilitate his fortunes, Grant accepted an offer from Mark Twain, then a publisher, to publish his memoirs.

Soon after he started the work, he learned that he had inoperable throat cancer, and the book became a battle against time.

His debts weighing heavily on him, Grant dictated to a stenographer, while his family researched documents to reinforce his battlefield recollections.

His weight declined to 130 from over 200, and he was on morphine for the pain. His voice all but gone, he used it only to dictate his book. He wrote his answers to questions.

Finally it was done. He allowed himself to be carried upstairs to bed, and he was dead within days. In 11 months, he had dictated two volumes of over a quarter million words and already had orders for 50,000 sets, assuring royalties of over $200,000 before publication. Moved by his last effort, the public eventually produced $500,000 in royalties for the family.

The memoirs were classic, and without a Wall Street panic, they would never have been. The panic ran its course—as panics do—and the next wave of speculators and shysters entered the Street as they have always done.

CHAPTER 35

THE WITCH OF WALL STREET (1884)

Hetty Robinson began her investment education as a six-year-old by reading the financial pages of the paper to her blind grandfather. The grandfather, Gideon Howland, had extended the family fortune made from whaling. Whale oil was in demand for lamps through much of the 19th century.

Hetty Howland Robinson's mother, Abby Slocum Howland, married Edward Mott Robinson, who turned Abby's part of the family fortune ($40,000) into $5 million by his death in 1865. As an adolescent, Hetty followed Robinson around the docks while he conducted the whaling business, and thereby learned the finer points of business and money management. Upon his death, Hetty inherited $1 million directly and the income from another million held in trust. Her aunt Sylvia Ann Howland died two weeks later leaving another million in trust for Hetty.

At age 30, Hetty Robinson (Green), the witch of Wall Street, began her 50-year career in railroads, Chicago real estate, and the money market. With her fortune approaching $100 million at the turn of the 20th century, she was considered the richest woman in the world.

Hetty's parsimony was legendary. Her clothes were old and tattered, and she washed only the part of her skirts that dragged on the ground. She and a carriage driver spent most of one night searching for a lost 2 cent stamp that eventually turned up in her clothing.

But the real savings came in the way Hetty "did business." Before the panic of 1884, Hetty conducted business with the banking house of John J. Cisco and Son. Her father had stored his

FIGURE 35–1
The Witch of Wall Street, Hetty Green

Courtesy of Brown Brothers Stock Photos

wealth there during the Civil War, and Hetty had some $25 million in securities and cash deposited there.

Her husband, Edward H. Green, a millionaire in his own right, speculated heavily and was in trouble in 1884. He borrowed from Cisco on Hetty's collateral and without her knowledge. When she found out, she marched down to the bank and demanded her wealth. The bank refused until Green's debt was repaid, although Hetty alternately threatened and cried. Eventually she was forced to cover Green's debt, and she separated from both Green and the bank, putting both into bankruptcy.

Hetty loaded $25 million of securities into a cab and moved to Chemical National Bank—literally! For the next 25 years, she stored her money and her household goods—including dresses and a buggy—at the bank. She conducted business by sitting cross-legged on the cold stone floor by the circular staircase, with her trunks of securities and records protected by the stairs. Here she did business with the great and the not so great.

Hetty saved more than office space. This arrangement allowed her to circulate among the boardinghouses in Hoboken, New Jersey, paying minimal rent ($14 a month) and avoiding residence in New York, which would have taxed her wealth.

Hetty was a contemporary of the great railroad "operators" of postbellum Wall Street. She admired Russell Sage and, like him, was always ready to buy value and lend money during panics. Her posted rate of usury was 6 percent, the legal rate, but she was known to take all the market would bear. Hetty lent to the New York Central Railroad—a Vanderbilt property—and as much as $4.5 million to the city of New York, which helped keep the taxman off her doorstep.

Hetty battled lawyers and tax collectors constantly. It wasn't unusual to have one lawyer representing another one who couldn't collect his fee from Hetty. Hetty also used her wealth to punish those she didn't like. She warred with Colis P. Huntington over railroads for years and nearly destroyed him in 1899, when she found out he was borrowing from a particular bank. She then began making deposits to that bank until it had—and was lending—some $1.6 million. Huntington had use for every penny of it.

One day, when she was sure that Huntington was extended, she called on the bank for her money. Of course, the bank didn't have it and was forced to call Huntington's demand notes. His business survived—barely—but he died the next year, prompting the witch of Wall Street to dance with glee: "That old devil Huntington is dead. Serves him right!"

But there was a compassionate side to her personality, too. One of the consistent bears after the Civil War was a southerner named Addison Cammack. He held a seat on the New York Stock Exchange from 1876 to 1897. Mr. Cammack learned that the

Louisville and Nashville Railroad was going to reduce its dividend. Cammack sold great blocks of the stock as the price declined some 30 points. The dividend was cut, and Cammack started looking for stock to cover his short position and secure his million of profit. Hetty Green was a principal stockholder, and the floating supply had disappeared.

Cammack sent a polished broker to see Mrs. Green, asking not to be identified. But Hetty knew and suggested to the broker that Mr. Cammack come to the Chemical Bank to see her himself.

When Cammack arrived at the appointed hour, Hetty handed him a slip of paper with her itemized cost for 40,000 shares. "Just to be neighborly, if you will add $10 per share to my cost, then we can agree right quick!" Cammack was happy to be out of the corner, and Hetty had added $400,000 to her pile.

Hetty Green's advice on investing was quite simple. "There is no great secret to fortune making. All you have to do is buy cheap and sell dear, act with thrift and shrewdness and be persistent." If she had thought about it, she might add that it doesn't hurt to start young with an inherited fortune.

CHAPTER 36

THE SCRIBBLERS (1889)

"Another damned, thick square book! Always scribble, scribble, scribble! Eh! Mr. Gibbon?"

The Duke of Gloucester, upon receiving Edward Gibbon's
Decline and Fall of the Roman Empire, Volume II

The Spanish poet Don José de la Vega wrote *Confusion de Confusiones* (the worst of confusions) in 1688. This book describes the Amsterdam bourse as it existed then, concentrating on the games played by the speculators.

Thanks to de la Vega, we have a good description of options, futures, short selling, and stock-jobbing as it existed in the 17th century. Virtually all practices common to modern stock exchanges existed at that time. There were fixed terms for settlement and delivery and fixed brokerage fees. There was an official published price list showing both cash rates and futures. Loans were made against securities, just as they are today.

Up until 1672, official price records carried only the price of goods and exchanges, but after that the lists were supplemented with share prices and the lists became widely published in 1720.

In the United States, little note was taken of stock market activity until 1820, although day-by-day quotations on government scrip had been published since 1791. In that year, the *New York American* published a fierce paragraph on the progress of share gambling, regarding the fluctuation in price of United States Bank stock from 103 to 106 with "shorts" fearing a momentary "corner."

In 1822, the *New York Daily Advertiser* lists some prices and comments on the effect made on these prices by the "jobbers" of

'Change Alley in London. The Americans were learning from the English, who in turn had learned from the Dutch.

On March 10, 1815, the *New York Commercial Advertiser* carried the first complete price list of stocks ever published and that feature, plus some meager comment, was all that was available to business interests until well after the Civil War.

Men and Mysteries of Wall Street, published in 1872 by James K. Medberry, was one of the first books written about the American markets. It is classic in its description of the actual proceedings of the postbellum period.

In 1880, Charles Dow came to New York after reporting for a series of New England newspapers and began writing articles and editorials for the *New York Mail and Express.* Later he joined a news agency, where he met Edward Jones, and in 1882 the two of them began Dow Jones and Company. This company concentrated on "flimsies" or "slips," which were simple bulletins delivered to the financial institutions of Wall Street. The last bulletin of the day included a news sheet that led to *The Wall Street Journal.* On July 8, 1889, the first edition of *The Wall Street Journal* was published.

Dow was the editor, and his construction of an industrial stock index provided a valuable tool for measuring progress and interest in securities. He also wrote editorials on the general mechanics of market movement that have grown into a full-blown theory followed by technical market analysts to determine trend.

The Wall Street Journal is indispensable to the businessman today. Added to the Dow Jones umbrella was *Barron's,* a statistical publication started as a handbill by Clarence Barron in 1887. Barron was a statistician in Boston at the time.

The *Journal* was oriented to hard business news with some conservative comment thrown in for good measure.

By 1890, there were a number of statistical services, even though the list of all stocks traded took less than one full column of the newspapers. *Poor's Manual* was a standard source for railroad company details, along with Moody's in the industrial sector. The *Commercial and Financial Chronicle* was used much as *The Wall Street Journal* is today.

Richard D. Wyckoff started one of the first financial magazines in 1902, calling it *The Ticker.* He later changed the title to *The Magazine of Wall Street.* The work began as a house organ for the

brokerage that employed Wyckoff, featuring articles on speculation methods by prominent investors of that time. This monthly
publication soon spun off a technically based market advisory
letter called *The Trend Letter*. This was the first of many such
letters to come, advising subscribers when to buy and sell and
where to set stop loss orders to protect their principal. Wyckoff
claimed to have moved the market with his prognostications and to
have made fortunes for his subscribers. However, his wealth came
only after he sold his publication company in 1926.

By this time, there were a number of business publications.
Bertie Charles (BC) Forbes started his magazine (*Forbes*) in 1916.
Business Week came along in 1929, and *Fortune* a year later.
Malcolm S. Forbes took over *Forbes* after a semisuccessful run at
politics and has made *Forbes* into a prosperous and respected
"capitalist tool."

Today there are hundreds of market letters, by both institutions and individuals. Financial magazines and books abound, and
television and print news tell us much more than we need to know
about investment (speculation) possibilities. Scribble, scribble,
scribble . . . .

In the rush to keep the public informed, reporters have gone
beyond the simple reporting function to venture theory and opinion
of their own. They are very moral in their judgments against
wealth—at least until they are found to be unethical in their own
use of unpublished financial information. Buy a stock and then
recommend it, for example!

Andrew Carnegie was once taken to task by a reporter on his
inordinate wealth: "Mr. Carnegie, don't you think you should
distribute your wealth to the less fortunate of the world?" Carnegie
looked at him in disbelief and then instructed his secretary: "Get
me the latest figures on my wealth and world's population." When
the data were provided, Carnegie pulled the stump of a pencil from
his pocket, did some arithmetic on the back of an envelope and
then told the secretary: "Give this man 2 cents—that's his share of
my fortune!"

CHAPTER 37

THE MONEY KING (1891)

Radio skit:

MUGGER:

Your money or your life!
(Pause)

MUGGER:

Look, Bud, I said your money or your life!

JACK BENNY:

I'm thinking it over!

Jack Benny may have used Russell Sage as a role model. Sage was a parsimonious old millionaire who conducted the longest-running craps game in history. For 50 years he sold "privileges" (options) at the corner of Broad and Wall. He didn't invent the game, but he certainly refined it!

Options are contractual rights to buy or sell a commodity (goods, stocks, currencies, etc.) at a specified price by a specified date. It is a right, not an obligation, and the purchaser of the option pays for this "privilege." His loss is limited to the price of the option, and he has a chance for a significant profit with a relatively small amount of capital. The seller of the option has statistics in his favor, because most options expire unexercised and the seller pockets the premium.

Options originated in Holland after 1602 on the common stock of the Dutch East India Company and were widely employed during the tulip craze of 1636–37. Options on stocks were available in the United States in the early 19th century, but it wasn't until

FIGURE 37–1
Russell Sage and His Office (1890), Just before the Bombing

Courtesy of Brown Brothers Stock Photos

after the Civil War and during the railroad expansion that Russell
Sage raised it to an art form.

Russell Sage, the Money King, subscribed to the Horatio
Alger school of success with the time-tested principles of work and
sacrifice. At age 12, he was a clerk in his brother's store earning $4
per month. Years later, when he was worth more than $100 million,
he claimed to still have the first dollar earned at that job, which was
also the first dollar he had ever seen. When asked how he had made
his money, Sage replied: "I made my millions from maxims, chief

of which was the one my father favored, which went: 'any man can earn a dollar, but it takes a wise man to keep it!' "

By the time Sage was 18, he was buying, selling, and lending money to a select clientele that eventually supported his interest in politics. His loans were always secured by "collateral."

Elected to the 33rd Congress in 1852, Sage introduced the bill to preserve Mount Vernon, but spent most of his energy on the politics of railroad expansion. He was president of one line, vice president of another, and a director of Vanderbilt's New York Central. His political connections served him well in his later Wall Street and railroad career.

Turned out of Congress in 1857, Sage turned to Wall Street in the panic of that year with his "ready cash" and could be found at the corner of Broad and Wall participating in the money market. He perfected the system of "call loans" by issuing pasteboards, similar to pawn tickets, along with the money borrowed once the collateral, in the form of good securities, had been deposited in his office. More often than not, the money was not repaid, and Sage ended up with the securities. The natural extension of the business was to write privileges on the securities thus obtained.

Although the use of an option to buy a security (call) and the option to sell a security (put) were offered by others, Sage extended the process by inventing the "spread" and the "straddle." The straddle is a put and call at the same price, the spread is a put and call at different prices.

His contributions to this field and his ability to read fluctuations and set prices appropriately earned him the title "father of puts and calls" and "old straddle."

His business came as close to a sure thing as you ever get in financial affairs. Sage was a pillar of trust, remaining solvent through five panics and never reneging on a written contract, although he reluctantly paid out over $7 million against puts during the panic of 1884.

The reputation that Sage had for having $1 million in ready cash resulted in a robbery attempt and bombing in 1891. A young broker from Boston, in financial straits, came to the office at the corner of Broadway and Rector and invoked John D. Rockefeller's name to get an audience with Sage. When Sage appeared, he was handed a note demanding $1.2 million under threat of dropping 10 pounds of dynamite.

Sage read the note twice and with his "customer's smile" in place began edging toward the door. The mad bomber challenged him by pulling a pistol. Sage told him he had to go to the vault and kept moving toward the door. The dynamite exploded as the septuagenarian Sage dove headfirst through the door.

Sage's personal secretary was blasted out the window and died later. Several clerks were injured as was Sage. The offices were destroyed, and Sage's papers drifted down among the tombstones in Trinity graveyard.

The extortionist was blown to bits. All that was found of him was a suspender button from Brooks Brothers that provided identification—and his head!

Sage took to his bed, and police inspectors carried a wicker basket with the broker's remains into Sage's bedroom for confirmation. Sage calmly pronounced the head to be the guilty one.

When the news first reached the floor of the New York Stock Exchange, it was rumored that Sage had been killed and a flash panic ensued. When a corrected report arrived, a major rally broke out. Russell Sage's health was important to Wall Street.

Russell Sage was far from an admirable character. His stinginess was legendary. He ate lunch each day at the expense of Western Union (he was a director), and he pocketed pads and pencils after each directors' meeting. He either rode the Manhattan Elevated train free (director with a lifetime pass), or he would share a carriage with Jay Gould in order to stick him with the fare. Still, he never failed to step into the breach during panic with his millions in hand.

Puts and calls were upgraded to an efficient market by their incorporation on the Chicago Board Options Exchange in 1973. The market now sets their prices accurately with only the commissions detracting from a fair game. Russell Sage is the only person known to have built his fortune through the medium of "privileges," and he was able to set the odds. There is no evidence that anyone accepting the unfavorable odds ever accumulated any significant wealth, but the mechanism still exists for anyone wanting to try their luck.

CHAPTER 38

THE BUCKET SHOP (1892)

"So gambling is illegal and the lottery's a flop, don't despair, just trot down to the old bucket shop."

In the London of Charles Dickens, drunks would visit the public houses with buckets in hand, begging the dregs from the bottom of each barrel of ale. When the buckets were full, these entrepreneurs would gather to rest and systematically empty their containers. The rooms where they met were termed *bucket shops*, and stock brokers were quick to accuse their rivals of operating offices like bucket shops. The term was transported to the United States and applied to a set of pseudo-brokerages that had sprung up all over the country.

The great American speculator at the turn of the 20th century was Jesse Laurston Livermore. As a child, Livermore had marked quotations on a brokerage chalkboard, and by the age of 15, he had accumulated his first thousand dollars by frequenting the bucket shops on his lunch break.

The bucket shop accepted margins of $1 per share (most shares traded near par of $100) allowing you to "buy" or "sell" stocks, although no actual stock transactions occurred. In effect, the bucket shop bet against you, counting on the thin margin and commissions to provide its profits. The quotation board was used as dice would be in other games of chance.

When you placed your margin, you were given a color-coded slip (buy or sell) indicating the stock involved, with the date, time, and last published quotation. You also paid a commission of ¼ point. When you were ready to close your position, the slip and the latest quotation completed the process. Again there was a ¼ point commission. Anytime the stock moved beyond a given limit against you, the margin was collected and the slip was worthless.

Livermore's uncanny ability to read the tape and bet successfully on fluctuations, eventually betrayed him as the bucket shops denied his play or charged exorbitant premiums and set a higher margin requirement. At age 21, he was forced to move on to Wall Street, where he became a millionaire four times with bankruptcies in between. The practice of bucket shops was made illegal by the Securities Exchange Act of 1934.

The physical presence of the bucket shop is part of the market's colorful past. However, the function is alive and has moved uptown to the respectable brokerage firms. The modest game of puts and calls sashayed into the main casino with establishment of the Chicago Board Options Exchange in 1973. This game maintains a thin thread of credibility because the underlying stocks are actually bought and sold 15 percent of the time, thus options are considered a desirable mechanism for hedging investments. Mathematically, this won't wash for the individual investor, as the negative expectation of options puts a drag on the individual's portfolio.

In 1982, the casino expanded again to allow trading of stock indexes in the futures markets. This means you can bet on the future direction of the market as represented by a computed index for as little as 5 percent margin and for as long as the 90 days' duration of the contract.

There are no actual stocks bought or sold, no dividends paid, and the limited time frame of the contract essentially removes the positive bias that inflation gives to most markets. In essence, we have what the statisticians would call a fair game, were it not for the commissions to be paid.

However, you must pay the commissions and you are now playing in the broker's casino. He owns the roulette wheel, and you are eventually subjected to empty pockets. If you do win, there are taxes to be paid. Congress may have outlawed the bucket shop, but it's OK now with Uncle Sam as a limited partner.

There are ways for the individual investor to make money in the securities markets. Buying value and holding long term while collecting dividends has been proven over and over again. Conversely, few Jesse Livermores survive the bucket shops after sustained play. Livermore himself would not be able to successfully employ his methods today because of increased commission percentages and more efficient markets.

The institutional traders may be well served by index futures to insure against sudden depreciation of their portfolio and to make arbitrage operations possible. Of course, it also creates market volatility around expiration dates, and the average professional doesn't do as well as the average stock.

But, for the individual, the bucket shop is back. It is a game operated every bit as honestly and circumspectly as the casinos in Las Vegas, but it also has the same inevitable result. Caveat emptor! Let the investor beware!

CHAPTER 39

THE NORTHERN PACIFIC CORNER (1901)

By the advent of the Civil War, railroads were spreading all over the country, like measles at a boarding school. At least this was Daniel Drew's observation of the great rail expansion. On July 2, 1864, both the Union Pacific and the Northern Pacific railroads received their charters.

The Northern Pacific was authorized to build a line from Lake Superior to an unspecified port on the Pacific Ocean. The first president was Josiah Perham, who attempted to sell shares to the everyday worker, and consequently the railroad didn't go anywhere very fast.

Jay Cooke, the Philadelphia banker known for financing the Civil War, bought the languishing line and laid the first track in Minnesota in 1870, reaching the Red River and North Dakota early in 1871.

The line was extended to Bismarck when the financial panic of 1873 bankrupted Jay Cooke and Company. The Northern Pacific followed shortly thereafter.

Before work was halted, surveyors had been introduced to Sitting Bull and the Hunkpapa Indians. By 1873, the army, with Lieutenant Colonel George Armstrong Custer in charge of the Seventh Cavalry, had been called in and was skirmishing with Sitting Bull.

Henry Villard, owner of the Oregon Central Railroad, now bought controlling interest in the Northern Pacific, and by 1883, it had reached Helena, Montana, to join his Oregon Central to the coast. The opening was a grand affair with Generals Grant and Sheridan as well as Sir Sitting Bull, down from Canada, present.

FIGURE 39–1
J. Pierpont Morgan

Courtesy of Brown Brothers Stock Photos

Custer had been dead for seven years, and when Sitting Bull fled to Canada, he was knighted—much to the chagrin of the United States.

Even as the completion of the line was being celebrated, the stock was falling in a depressed market, ending in receivership again.

The railroad stood still until Villard came back as a majority shareholder six years later. This prosperity lasted only until 1893, when in the panic of that year, it returned to the receiver.

Meanwhile, Jim Hill and the Great Northern Railroad weathered the financial panic—thanks to good management—and by 1895, he was working with J. P. Morgan on a rescue plan for the Northern Pacific, quietly buying stock in the open market.

Edward H. Harriman, a Wall Street broker turned railroader, was a power in eastern railroads and had recently bought control of the Illinois Central and was looking west at the Union Pacific, which was being reorganized after the 1893 depression.

The firm of Kuhn, Loeb, and Company, headed by Jacob Schiff, soon found Harriman to be opposing its activity in reorganizing the Union Pacific. The firm invited him to join, and he was made chairman of the executive committee of the new Union Pacific. By 1900, he had controlling interest in the stock, and the Union Pacific was looking to secure control of a competing line, the Chicago, Burlington and Quincy (Burlington).

Hill and Morgan also wanted the Burlington to provide an eastern terminus for the Northern Pacific. Both parties went after the Burlington with a vengeance. Jacob Schiff formed a syndicate with George Gould (Jay's son) and Rockefeller interests and apparently had control by buying up a majority of the common stock on the open market. The floating supply had certainly run dry.

In the meantime, Morgan and Hill were negotiating directly with the Burlington's directors and soon had controlling interest in the line.

Schiff and Harriman were up to the challenge and decided that if the mother wouldn't part with the pup, they would buy the mother instead. They quietly began buying Northern Pacific stock. When they had acquired nearly half the common and more than half the preferred, they informed Morgan they had control. However, Morgan knew of a clause in the bylaws that allowed a vote of the common stock to redeem the preferred, so he went to the open market, soaked up the floating supply of the common, and scheduled a vote to redeem the preferred stock for the following January.

All the activity in the common raised the price from 112 to 149 and attracted short sellers. They soon discovered—to their horror—that they couldn't cover. Morgan had created an unintended corner. On May 9, 1901, it all came to the flashpoint. The price of Northern Pacific common stock began at 170, 20 minutes later was at 205, then 225, 230, 280, 300, 650, 700, and finally $1,000 on consecutive trades.

Call money jumped to 70 percent, and the remainder of the market plummeted as stocks were sold indiscriminately to raise money. Union Pacific, for example, dropped 57 points, which was close to 50 percent. U.S. Steel dropped from 53 on May 7 to 24 on May 9 and recovered to 45 on May 10. At 2:30 P.M. the Hill and Harriman groups both offered to lend their stock to the shorts and relief was immediate. Call money dropped to 40 percent, then 6 percent, and finally 3 percent by the market close. The next day the shorts were allowed to settle at 150 per share and the panic was over.

Kuhn, Loeb, and Company did not have a voting majority, if the preferred were redeemed, but its current majority in both classes of stock gave it a decided legal advantage. Morgan and Hill did not want a prolonged legal battle, so a compromise was effected.

A new company, known as the Northern Securities Company, was organized as a holding company for all the stocks of all railroads owned by both factions. Both groups were equally represented on the board, and the most gigantic legal battle for a company ever staged in Wall Street was ended.

Corners are an unlikely event now because of the required delivery of all shares sold short and the enormous amount of capital needed to control. The Northern Pacific was the last one, and it was accidental.

CHAPTER 40

BIG STEEL (1901)

Three men dominated the business activity in the United States by the turn of the 20th century. John D. Rockefeller was a merchant turned oilman, and his giant Standard Oil had a virtual monopoly on the vast oil business. Andrew Carnegie had survived a major depression in 1893 and had, by far, the largest interest in steel production in America. The third giant of industry was J. P. Morgan, who controlled a vast banking and railroad empire.

All three got their start during the Civil War. Carnegie was western division manager of the Pennsylvania Railroad when the fighting started. He was assigned the job of restoring track and reestablishing communications that the rebels had destroyed. In 1864, he started the Cyclops Iron Works and in 1865, just before Lincoln's assassination, resigned from the Pennsylvania Road to build his iron—later steel—business.

Rockefeller was in the produce commission business building his small fortune from rising commodity prices during the Civil War. In August 1859, oil had been discovered in western Pennsylvania, and Rockefeller had been closely following developments there. In 1861, he and a partner developed a refinery in Cleveland and were processing the oil. Soon Rockefeller traded his interest in commodities for the partner's interest in oil.

J. Pierpont Morgan had a father who was a leading banker and a millionaire. J. P. had a classic education in the United States and Europe and was thoroughly prepared for his role as principal banker for the railroad, oil, and steel interests. He began his career by selling defective rifles to the Union army during the war and, by 1869, was lending to and controlling a number of small railways. In 1879, he organized a syndicate to buy Vanderbilt's New York Central stock and emerged as the dominant U.S. banker.

Morgan became so central to money lending that the federal government had to borrow $50 million from him in 1894 to buy foreign gold. In the panic of 1907, set off by bank failures, J. P. Morgan entered, in its extremity, and formed a syndicate to pool their money and prop up each bank as it was subjected to runs.

By 1901, Andrew Carnegie, John D. Rockefeller, and Morgan were the three largest interests in the steel industry. Rockefeller controlled the Mesabi iron range and offered Carnegie $100 million for his company, but the deal failed when Carnegie called for cash. Morgan was busy merging steel companies and announced he would compete in products previously bought from Carnegie. Carnegie countered by entering the bridge and tube business, where Morgan held a monopoly. As an afterthought, he stated he would discontinue use of Morgan's railroads and build his own.

Morgan's bluff was called, and Charles Schwab was asked to negotiate with Carnegie. The price of $492 million came back to Morgan, and he accepted without a blink.

Years later, Morgan and Carnegie were on the same ship bound for Europe, having breakfast, and talk got around to the steel merger. Carnegie ventured an opinion to J. P.: "Do you know, Mr. Morgan, I have been thinking it over, and I find that I made a mistake. I should have asked for another $100 million for those properties." Morgan was just as open with his reply: "If you had, I should have paid it." And Carnegie was so upset at that answer that he couldn't finish his toast and marmalade.

Morgan came up with $21 million to organize the United States Steel Corporation in the state of New Jersey. Morgan then hired Jim Keene to sell securities, and a billion-dollar corporation was sold to the general public, even though it was worth only a fraction of that in asset value. Offered at 24, it went to 55 under Keene's skillful promotion, only to slide below 9 three years later. Daniel Drew would have been green with envy at the successfully watered operation sold to the public.

Morgan loomed larger than life itself. He was the center of all financial transactions and dominated each. He was never challenged more than once and rarely bested. Even the gods favored him; one of his companies owned the Titanic, and a stateroom had been set aside for Morgan's personal use. He had been scheduled to make the maiden voyage in 1912 but decided to stay in Europe instead.

Morgan exuded such an aura of invincibility that the world was shocked at his passing in 1913. He left an estate—mostly art treasures—valued at $77.5 million. This prompted the admiring John D. Rockefeller to come out from behind his own $500 million pile and comment: "And to think that he wasn't even a rich man!"

CHAPTER 41

BARBED WIRE AND BET-A-MILLION (1901)

John W. Gates was a wire drummer in Illinois earning $30 per month in 1876. Business was bad and his company was trying to open up the market with cattlemen in Texas, so Gates went to San Antonio to sell barbed wire to the ranchers.

The warehouses were full of wire, and the conventional sales approach only brought laughs from the cattlemen. "We like you, Gates, but your wire ain't any good." Gates spent the days trodding the dusty ranges and the evenings honing his skills in the gambling houses.

Always on the lookout for the big idea, Gates saw the huge crowds drawn by a medicine show in Military Plaza and suddenly had his plan. He rounded up 60 of the meanest looking longhorns he could find and staged a rodeo in the plaza. The show finale was a demonstration of his barbed wire, and Gates introduced it thusly: "This is the best fencing in the world, it's light as air, stronger than whiskey, cheaper than dirt!" Forty longhorns were herded into the corral and then stampeded against the wire. The wire held, the cattle backed off, the ranchers bought, and Gates was on his way.

Gates soon became an independent wire manufacturer and spent the next 20 years organizing other independents into what eventually became the American Steel and Wire Company, an enormous trust with a capitalization of $90 million.

After his success with wire, Gates had moved into Illinois Steel, which was second only to the Carnegie interests after 1893. By 1898, J. P. Morgan's interest in steel had brought Illinois Steel into the Federal Steel Trust, and Gates had been eased out. Gates's response was to expand American Steel and Wire.

By 1900, the wire and nail business was booming, and Gates was spending much of his time holding court in Astor's Waldorf hotel. He entertained himself and his followers by betting huge sums on random events such as which of two flies would depart first from a sugar cube or which of two raindrops would reach the bottom of a glass pain first.

One evening, in the lobby of the hotel crowded with Wall Street traders, he remarked loudly to a friend that he planned to close his steel mill because business was so poor. He also happened to be short of his stock and did close temporarily, while the stock dropped from the 60s into the 30s. He closed his short position, went long, and calmly opened his mills after announcing business had suddenly improved.

Quite a stir was created by Gates's operation, and he decided it was time to vacation in Europe. By this time, he was a regular fixture at the racetracks, and in England, he bet $70,000 on Royal Flush, winning some $600,000 on one race. This touched off rumors that he had bet an even million, and the turf writers announced that in America he was known as Bet-a-Million.

J. P. Morgan was consolidating steel companies in 1901, and Gates's interests in American Steel and Wire were traded for securities in the newly formed United States Steel Corporation. Gates wanted a wider role in the new organization but was denied by Morgan, who didn't trust him. In retaliation, Gates decided to irritate Morgan by crimping his railroad expansion. To accomplish this, he quietly bought control of the Louisville and Nashville Railroad.

Morgan was furious. Gates had bought his shares around $100, and Morgan dispatched Charles Schwab, president of U.S. Steel, to offer Gates $150. Gates refused. Morgan became more agitated at the potential to sabotage his southern rail system. Finally Morgan sent one of his partners to see Gates at 1:30 in the morning. Gates was in flowered pajamas and a red robe. After an hour of fruitless negotiation, Gates gave Morgan's man a take-it-or-leave-it offer. The market price of his shares plus a $10 million bonus. Morgan's partner was under orders to complete the deal, and so Gates's terms were accepted. Although Gates tried, he was never able to best Morgan again.

Without a company to run, Gates set up shop in the Waldorf

and speculated on the Street. In May 1901, Morgan was battling Harriman for control of Northern Pacific Railroad. Gates and his friends were following the action, buying shares as the prices swirled upward. They spent their time eating the hotel's rich food, singing Morgan's favorite hymns (derisively), and playing poker and bridge.

All this activity kept their telegrapher so busy he had to pack his lunch. In his box lunch was a huge slab of lemon pie. Gates and his crowd looked so hungrily at the pie that the next day he brought them a whole pie.

"Just like my mother used to make," said Gates. "We must do something for a lady that can make pie like that!" So Gates and his buddies bought 100 shares of "Nipper" (Northern Pacific) at 113 ½ and credited it to "A. G. Pymacher" (a good pie maker). The telegrapher was to have the profit when he decided to sell the stock. That day Northern Pacific was 120, the next day 130. The telegrapher was sweating, but Gates and his friends offered no advice. On May 8, the stock was sold at 130, and the telegrapher pocketed $1,500 for his lemon pie. The next day, May 9, the stock sold as high as $1,000, which would have been a potential profit of $86,500 for the exchange of a lemon pie. A classic case of selling too soon!

Everything Gates touched turned to gold. In 1900, he was approached about an interest in a $50,000 oil exploration company. Gates was interested only if he could have 51 percent. He promised ports and transportation if the wells produced and was sold controlling interest. On January 10, 1901, the spindletop well blew and the Texas Company (TEXACO) was on its way.

The betting man died in 1911 with his fortune intact. His shares of Texas Company and a host of metals and railroads were worth nearly $50 million. Morgan died two years later with a fortune only slightly larger. Not bad for a barbed wire salesman.

PART 5

THE GLOBAL STREET (1907–1939)

PART 5

THE GLOBAL STREET
(1907–1939)

CHAPTER 42

THE GRAIN APHIS (1907)

With the railroads providing access to the farmlands of the Midwest, Chicago soon became an agricultural hub with its elevators, railyards, warehouses, and port facilities attracting more and more farmers to the city with their products. However, the city was without a central trading facility and the farmer had to go from merchant to merchant seeking the best price for his crops. Prices fluctuated dramatically, and there were bitter disputes between buyer and seller.

In 1848, 82 Chicago merchants solved the problem by organizing the Chicago Board of Trade, which has had 13 homes since then, including the one on LaSalle Street, occupied since 1930. The previous building existed from 1883 until 1929 and was the scene of some classic battles in the grain pits. It was to this arena that Arthur Cutten came in 1890, from Guelph, Canada, with a $90 stake and his bicycle.

After 18 months of odd jobs, Cutten found himself working for a broker in the wheat pit of the Chicago Board of Trade, converting currencies for foreign invoices. Even though the watchword in commodities speculation is secrecy, Cutten was able to learn by observing the great speculators in action.

Armour and Company was the dominant force in the pits. P. D. Armour would ride down to the exchange each morning in a buggy drawn by a magnificent team of horses to watch his team of brokers in action. Sometimes at a breakfast counter, Cutten would sit next to a fierce old fellow in ministerial costume who was the legend of LaSalle Street. This was Benjamin P. Hutchinson ("Old Hutch"), who had taken millions out of the grain pits, but in his declining years was returning his wealth to the market, as had so many others both before and since.

FIGURE 42–1
The Grain Aphis

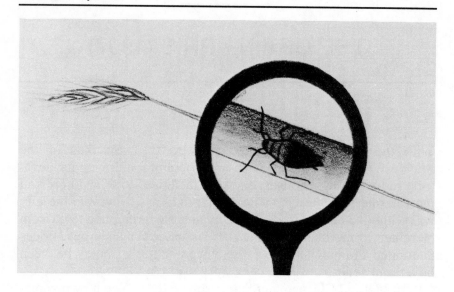

Cutten's role model was Jim Patten. Patten and his partner would sit with straight-back chairs tilted back against a pillar near the corn pit, nibbling a stem of grain, observing the action.

Patten and his brother, George, were fundamentalists and went to great extremes to gather information. They were also always quick to change direction if new information implied they were wrong.

By 1896, Cutten had convinced his brokerage firm that he should be a pit trader, and he soon was making profitable trades in corn for A. S. White and Company, along with "scalping" (speculating on small changes in price) successfully on his own.

Soon he had enough of a stake to resign from A. S. White and go into the pits on his own. He adhered to the Patten philosophy of following fundamentals by studying weather, insects, transportation, planting statistics, and so on. Every night he went home with weather charts under his arm, and he had an extensive chart of historical grain prices prepared by George Broomhall, the

British statistical authority on grain. It traced the effects of war on grain prices and was of particular interest to Cutten in 1914.

But in 1907, Cutten was working on his first major wheat deal, and it was the year of the green bug plague. The green bug was a grain aphis.

The grain aphis was a plant louse normally held in check by a tiny black insect that deposited eggs in the bodies of the green bugs. These eggs hatched and fed on the internals of the grain aphis. These black bugs were active only when the temperature went above 56 degrees Fahrenheit. Anything less than that, and the green bug breeds freely.

In 1907, a cool spring allowed the grain aphis to multiply unmolested. On the floor of the Chicago Board of Trade were bottles with these bugs and blades of wheat. When Cutten saw the grain aphis suck the blades of young and tender wheat, he would hustle back to the wheat pit to buy some more.

By 1924, Cutten was a major force in Chicago and on his way to accumulating 3 million bushels of wheat. In the process, he caught J. Ogden Armour of Armour and Co. (meats) short of wheat. Cutten had filled the elevators with wheat on cash delivery, and no space was available. Contracts called for delivery in the public elevators of Chicago. Armour could find no place to accept his delivery and was in trouble.

When in trouble, the bears have always resorted to historical precedent and plead for the rules of the game to be changed. Armour persuaded the Board of Trade to allow emergency delivery of wheat in railroad cars west of Chicago. This meant Cutten would stand a demurrage cost of $39,000 per day. He decided to stand pat and pay the charges, but smaller speculators began to liquidate. Wheat dropped 30 cents and Cutten took a drubbing.

In 1925, Cutten cornered wheat again, buying at $1.32 and selling at $2. This time he came away with $10 million in profit and a reputation of legendary proportions. That year he paid over $400,000 in taxes, and in 1926, government reporting requirements drove Cutten from the pits forever and onto Wall Street, where he increased his fortune during the great bull market of the 20s.

After retiring from active speculation, Cutten gave his story to the *Saturday Evening Post* in 1932. The strategy that emerges from that biography highlights the following principles.

1. Cutten worked hard at fundamentals.
2. He waited for undervalued situations.
3. He worked the calculus of probability (his term).
4. He played the long side of the market.
5. He accumulated a position slowly and systematically.
6. He let his profits run.
7. He concentrated on one commodity or stock at a time.

When the old building on LaSalle Street was torn down in 1929, Cutten was presented with a couple of the stained glass windows that filtered light into the old facility. Somehow that wasn't enough, so he asked for and received the two sculptures from over the doorway representing commerce and labor. He had the 16 tons of stone and pigeon deposits transported to his farm 20 miles west of Chicago, where they laid prone and hidden in his hollyhock garden for the rest of his life.

CHAPTER 43

COMMON STOCKS FOR THE COMMON MAN (1915)

In 1885, Arthur Housman and John Burrill formed the brokerage firm of Burrill and Housman. In 1890, Burrill withdrew, and soon after Housman took his brother Clarence and Bernard Baruch into the business. Both were 21 years old. Clarence was made a partner, and Baruch became a $3 per week clerk. It took Bernard six years to be elevated to partner. By 1901, Baruch had made his fortune and brought his brother Saling into the firm. On the day of the Northern Pacific corner (May 9, 1901), Edward Allen Pierce started with A. A. Housman as a clerk.

By 1903, Bernard Baruch had other interests and had left the firm. In 1907, Arthur Housman died, leaving the firm to Clarence Housman and Saling Baruch. In the panic of that same year, Charles Merrill and Edward Lynch came to town. Meeting at the 23rd Street YMCA, the two men formed a lifelong friendship and, after starting separate careers, formed the partnership of Merrill Lynch and Company in 1915. Pierce was elevated to partner at A. A. Housman that same year.

Lynch started as a salesman of soda fountain equipment. Once sent to collect an overdue bill of $122.80, Lynch was warned by the debtor that he didn't have enough in the bank to cover the debt. Lynch insisted on a check for the full amount anyway. When Eddie arrived at the bank, he was told that the account was $8 short. Lynch promptly deposited $8 of his own money into the client's account and, moving to another teller's window, cashed the client check.

Both A. A. Housman and Company and Merrill Lynch and Company prospered during the roaring 20s, with A. A. Housman and Company becoming E. A. Pierce and Company in 1927 after a series of acquisitions.

As the 1920s progressed, Charles Merrill was among those that sensed the impending storm. He wrote his customers in March 1928 telling them to sell enough securities to get out of debt. The research department thought he was out of his mind, but Merrill insisted on the letter going out.

At the end of 1928, Merrill expressed his concern about excessive speculation to the lame-duck President Coolidge, asking him to join the firm to speak against overextension of credit and excessive speculation. The president turned him down by recalling President Grant's disastrous venture into finance.

Finding little agreement and beset by self-doubt, Merrill was advised to see a psychiatrist. Explaining his concerns to the good doctor, he was listened to patiently. On the next visit, the psychiatrist started the session by showing Merrill a set of closed-out brokerage statements. The doctor had sold out and proceeded to give Charles his diagnosis: "Charlie, if you're crazy, then so am I."

Merrill's partners still weren't convinced. Early in 1929, Merrill wrote them an impassioned letter, pleading for his indulgence by turning a large portion of the firm's securities into cash. The $20 million reluctantly raised by the partners served him well in the aftermath of the crash.

In 1930, the brokerage business was turned over to Pierce, while Merrill Lynch and Company concentrated on investment banking.

The brokerage business was tough during Depression years, and E. A. Pierce and Company, with 10 percent of the total, was no exception. In 1940, Winthrop Smith, as a partner of Pierce and a previous partner of Merrill, arranged a merger, where Merrill was to be in charge. Eddie Lynch had died in 1938. Before long, they had absorbed the firm of Fenner and Beane, and the new firm was named Merrill Lynch, Pierce, Fenner and Beane. The founder Beane was dead, and when his son failed to be elected president of the merged firm in 1957, he withdrew himself and his name from the company. Early in 1958, Winthrop Smith replaced him as principal in the corporate title.

When Charlie Merrill assumed command in 1940, he stated his

intention to bring Wall Street to Main Street. In that same year, Elmo Roper was commissioned by the New York Stock Exchange to find out how the general public viewed Wall Street. The answer that came back was that Wall Street wasn't trusted. Merrill took the report seriously and decided to go openly and directly to the public to improve the image.

First, he changed the brokerage offices, making them more accessible and comfortable. Then he started a program of educational advertising. Louis Engel's *How to Buy Stocks*—a classic primer—came out of the research department. Merrill's slogan was "investigate, then invest." The research department turned out an enormous volume of material.

Next, Merrill turned his salesmen into investment counselors (account executives). They were placed on salary, giving the perception of being there to help the customer. The move had significant advertising value. By 1950, the firm had 150,000 accounts and was spending more than $1 million per year on research and market letters. The middle class of America was attracted to the securities markets, with over 11,400 brokers in the industry serving that interest in 1950. In 1988, that figure approached 100,000 in the United States. Research and information distribution in the industry has grown proportionally.

In 1973, Merrill Lynch and Company led the effort for negotiated commissions. Along with other brokerage firms, Merrill Lynch sought more institutional business and wanted to acquire it by negotiating fees. In 1971, the Securities and Exchange Commission ruled that fees could be settled by negotiation for any trade involving $500,000 or more.

On May 1, 1975, fixed rates were abolished on all trades, and the free market was allowed to hold sway. At first, only the institutions benefited because the small investor saw his rates rise. The buttonwood agreement had called for ¼ of 1 percent, the railroading period saw the standard at ⅛ of 1 percent, and Henry Clews dropped it briefly to ¹⁄₁₆ of 1 percent while breaking into the business in 1857. Even though rates varied, the average investor could expect 2 percent or more after May 1, 1975.

But then the free market principle took hold! Discount brokers appeared, offering to buy or sell without the expensive frills of advice, research, and plush offices. The rates in 1988 are as much as 70 percent lower than the full service firms, even though discount houses offer all the mechanics and products.

Merrill Lynch and Company is still the world's largest brokerage firm. You'd think a company that large could afford to put a comma in the name between Merrill and Lynch. Why is it missing? In the early days of the Merrill and Lynch partnership, an order of stationery came back with the comma missing. The young, economy-minded partners decided to use the letterheads anyway. Later Merrill stated that if he had finished college he would have known more about punctuation. Besides, what was good enough for J. P. Morgan (Drexel Morgan), was good enough for Charlie Merrill.

What was good enough for Charlie Merrill and Eddie Lynch is good enough for the world's largest brokerage firm, and the common is still missing in Merrill Lynch and Company.

CHAPTER 44

LORD OF THE CURRENCY
(1919)

Consider the following scenario: It is morning in London, and a man in his late 30s is awake, but still in bed. He's on the phone with his broker in "The City" making decisions on large speculations for himself, his university, and a syndicate he advises.

This man is a world-famous economist with two acclaimed books to his credit, college bursar and don, government official and adviser, land baron, and wealthy investor. This is John Maynard Keynes—Lord Keynes—whose general theory of economics still dominates economic policies of major nations some 60 years after espousal and may continue to affect economic thought for years to come.

This is the picture painted for economics students—the brilliant, famous economist, married to a beautiful Russian ballerina, adviser to kings and presidents, and able to pile up a fortune speculating in currencies, commodities, and stocks for himself and Cambridge University in his spare time. It's the stuff dreams are made of, but there is another side to the story.

Keynes came from distinguished ancestry. His progenitors were people of education and influence, and his parents had the first marriage allowed between two teaching fellows at Cambridge. Maynard Keynes was the first born of this couple and much was given and expected of him. He graduated from Eton, the famous prep school on the Thames, and was elected to King's College (Cambridge) on a scholarship in mathematics and classics. In 1906, Keynes took the civil service exam and went to work for the India office. Two years later, he applied for a fellowship in mathematics at King's College, but was not selected.

Shortly after this, he was offered a fellowship to teach general economics, a position he retained until the end of his life.

One of his courses consisted of a weekly lecture on Indian currency and finance. His specialty soon became money, credit, and prices. During this period, he was also writing—particularly on probability and his first book *Indian Currency and Finance.*

When World War I broke out in 1914, a financial panic was feared, and Keynes was hired by the Treasury as a monetary expert. His first effort was to convince Lloyd George to maintain the gold standard. By war's end, he was firmly entrenched in Treasury and being sent abroad on a variety of financial matters. When a peace conference was arranged for Paris, Keynes was sent to represent the Treasury department of England.

After the conference, Keynes resigned from the Treasury and wrote *The Economic Consequences of the Peace.* The book was enormously popular—possibly because of the personality profiles he painted of Lloyd George, Woodrow Wilson, and Georges Clemenceau. His central thesis was that Germany was being asked to pay reparations that were unreasonable and uncollectable.

Walter Lippmann used Keynes's work in serial form, and Macmillan published the book with Keynes assuming the production expense and paying the publisher a 10 percent royalty. The work was done in Edinburgh, and the ship carrying it to London was wrecked. Two thousand copies of *The Economic Consequences of the Peace* washed up on the coast of Denmark. These were sold at public auction there. Eventually the book sold some 140,000 copies and was translated into a number of languages.

While Keynes was working on his book, he embarked on a new career in currency speculation. Based on his experience in the Treasury and insights on postwar Germany, he became bullish on the dollar and bearish on the European currencies, taking a 10 percent margin position on a variety of currencies. Soon he was making big profits, confident of his ability to see the economics of the situation better than the average investor.

In April 1920, Keynes viewed the need for more credit for Germany as a reason to take a bearish position on the mark. It had been falling steadily, but now reacted, and between April and May, Keynes lost some 13,125 pounds for himself and 8,498 pounds for his syndicate. The brokerage firm called for 7,000 pounds margin, and he was able to meet it only by a 5,000-pound loan from an admirer and a 1,500-pound advance on his book. By his own admission, he had been bankrupt.

In 1921, after restoring his finances through his writing, Keynes returned to speculation in commodities and securities, all on a margin basis.

From 1924 to 1937, he turned 57,797 pounds into 506,450 and established his reputation as a great speculator. This is a compounded rate of just over 17 percent annually, and while good, does not measure up to the longer record of the much more conservative Warren Buffett.

Keynes's official biographer reported that he gave up speculation in 1937 because he was ill. But then he had been ill off and on all his life, and he was well enough to spend nine more years influencing economics and politics. A more recent biography notes that he lost heavily in American securities in the 1937 market, and that may have put him into speculator's retirement. One bankruptcy he had survived, but a second might mar the reputation of the world's greatest economist.

Like many of the great financiers, Keynes was bold in large matters, always ready to risk large sums in support of a thesis. On small matters, he was very conservative. His friends used to complain about the meager meals they were served, laughing about passing the grouse around the table to pick the bones clean.

Once while Maynard and a friend were on vacation in Algiers, they had their shoes polished by native boys. Keynes underpaid the boys and was stoned in return. His friend suggested that he give them more to calm their wrath. To which John Maynard Keynes, the world's greatest economist, replied; "I will not be a party to debasing the currency."

CHAPTER 45

BOMBING THE STREET (1920)

On September 16, 1920, a rusty old wagon pulled by a dark bay horse rolled down Wall Street toward Trinity Church. It was just before noon when the wagon parked in front of the assay office, and the driver joined the crowd on the sidewalk.

Suddenly, there was a bluish white flash of light accompanied by a violent explosion and a mushroom-shaped cloud of yellowish green smoke. The air was filled with dust, and the street was littered with glass, stone, and the blood of the dead and dying.

Thirty-three people were killed and over 200 were injured. The interior of the world's financial citadel, the J. P. Morgan Company, was destroyed, with one killed and dozens hurt. Windows were smashed for blocks around, and an iron slug had been driven through the windows of the Banker's Club on the 34th floor of the Equitable Building.

Across "The Corner" from the blast was the excavation pit that was to become the annex of the New York Stock Exchange. Next to this, on Broad, were the Corinthian pillars of the exchange, behind which a day of trading at good volume was under way. A crash of the type unfamiliar to brokers was heard, followed by a shower of glass as the windows were blown out. The large crowd around the Reading Railroad post moved to the edge of the room, lest the dome should fall. The president of the exchange calmly remarked to one of the traders, "I guess it's about time to ring the gong," and mounting the rostrum, did just that to conclude the day's trading. The next day, prices opened as if nothing had happened.

This mystery bombing of the financial district was never solved, but credit is generally assigned to communist (Bolshevik) interests. The FBI conducted exhaustive investigations, tracing the

FIGURE 45–1

September 16, 1920, Looking West on Wall Street at the Corner of Broad and Wall after the Explosion

Courtesy of Brown Brothers Stock Photos

Note the Annex of the New York Stock Exchange being built in the top left corner of photo.

horse's shoes to a blacksmith. He remembered a Sicilian customer, but the trail ended there. One fragment of iron proved to be the knob of a safe that was identified as having gone to France during the war, returning to Hoboken afterward, but it had no further history. The "usual suspects" were rounded up, but that was fruitless.

A five-sheet note by the American anarchist fighters found in a nearby post box called for the freeing of political prisoners. This also yielded no further clues. The Bolsheviks were generally given credit, even as their influence was rapidly waning.

After the Russian Revolution of 1917, other countries suffered through a "Big Red Scare." Radical labor factions in the United States and Europe were conducting anarchist activities and arrests were common. The number of estimated communists in the United States was about 500,000 at the peak of the threat. Patriotic groups were called to arms, and skirmishes were common with strikes and riots and rulings against radicals.

The mayor of Seattle, stumping the nation warning of communist danger, had been sent a bomb through the mail as a warning that "big brother" was watching. The bomb was discovered and defused, but the next day the chairman of the Senate Immigration Committee, who had been outspoken on keeping the Bolsheviks out of the country, saw his maid's hands blown off when she opened the package intended for him.

The morning following that incident, a clerk in the New York Post Office was riding home in the subway when he read the news about the senator's maid; the description of the package reminded him of some he had handled that day. He left the train at the next stop and returned to the post office. The 16 packages were still on the shelf, with a Gimbels return address. They were addressed to J. P. Morgan, John D. Rockefeller, and a number of prominent people in finance and government. The packages had gone on the shelf because of insufficient postage. The police defused 16 bombs, and the comrades turned to other methods.

One of the 16 package bombs had been addressed to the United States attorney general. Several weeks later, the Reds took a more direct approach by bombing the front of his house in Washington. Two passersby were reduced to basic body parts, and Franklin D. Roosevelt, getting out of the car across the street, was lucky enough to be missed by the flying fragments. The attorney general and his family were in the back of the house and escaped again.

The attorney general responded by launching a Red hunt, rounding up hundreds of communists and deporting Russian-born suspects. Those with liberal or socialist inclinations turned back to capitalistic endeavors, and the speculators turned back to Wall Street.

The blast that reduced J. P. Morgan and Company offices to rubble and blew windows out of the New York Stock Exchange failed to as much as scar the statue of George Washington on the steps of the Subtreasury building even though it was as close as the house of Morgan was to the wagon. The Morgan facade was pockmarked by the flying shrapnel, and the scars remain there today to remind us of the explosion that rocked Wall Street nearly 70 years ago.

CHAPTER 46

THE KERB (1921)

On Monday, June 27, 1921, at 9 A.M., Edward McCormick, chairman of the New York Curb Exchange, strolled to the head of the curbstone brokers at Broad and Exchange Place. At his direction, the colorful band proceeded north to Wall Street and then west past Trinity Church and graveyard to the new quarters that is now the American Stock Exchange.

At 9:30 A.M., a after a presentation of keys, McCormick called for silence and pronounced: "The die is cast—the old order is gone forever!"

Back on Broad Street at 10 A.M., a group of some 50 street brokers resumed trading unlisted stocks in the open air as New Yorkers had been doing continuously for nearly 130 years.

Street trading has gone on as long as markets have existed, and in the United States, those origins coincide with the birth of our nation. When Hamilton's "stocks" were issued to redeem the Revolutionary War debt, they were first traded by auctioneers on the docks and then by brokers meeting under a buttonwood tree. As each group of brokers organized and moved indoors, a new or remnant group of curbstone brokers continued trading among themselves and for a select clientele in the street.

The curbstone brokers were always the havenots, excluded from the privileges and information of the formal exchanges, but instrumental in forcing the evolution of efficient markets as the system moved from auction to pits to specialist to computers and continuous markets. When the auction ceased on the floor of the New York Stock Exchange, then furious trading commenced in the streets. When the gong sounded on the Big Board at the end of the day, the "kerb" remained active into the night.

The curb exchanges were always forced to keep a wary eye on the organized exchanges because prices were set in those hallowed

FIGURE 46–1
Curb Market

Courtesy of Brown Brothers Stock Photos

Note the variety of hats and coats used for easy recognition within the crowd. Note also the interest in the upper levels of the buildings where incoming orders were relayed to the brokers through hand signals.

halls and knowing these prices was essential to the curbstone broker's survival. Thus, the street exchange could always be found in the vicinity of its indoor big brothers.

In 1837, the curbstone brokers rented a room next door to 'Change (as it was known), and they pried bricks out of the closet to see and hear what was happening on the floor of the exchange at the twice a day call-through auctions.

In 1857, activity accelerated as a flood of mining issues came on the street. The exchange at that time was located in the Dan Lord Building, and the keyhole was rented for $100 per day to the curb brokers.

As stocks were delisted or were unable to meet the requirements for listing on the New York Stock Exchange, curb activity
met the challenge and grew. When activity was stable and the
brokers flush, exchanges were organized with memberships and
the brokers moved indoors. In 1863, the Open Board was formed
and moved into dismal basement quarters known as the coal hole.
When the Erie Railroad stock was banned from the Big Board in
1869, the National Open Board was formed. This board was later
merged with the Big Board.

With each departure, a new group would spring up in its place
in the streets and with a new clientele, the American dream went
on. Trading started and ended by the governor banging on a swill
bucket as the colorfully clad brokers operated in all kinds of
weather at their lampposts. In 1921, when McCormick took his
brokers in from the cold, they were surprised to find their lamppost
stations duplicated on the floor of the new building. After operating
in the open air for so many years, the first winter brought on an
epidemic of colds as the brokers adjusted to their warm quarters.

With the advent of telephones, a new dimension was added to
curb operations. Buildings with ledges were at a premium to house
the brokers' offices and to relay messages to the brokers operating
in the streets. Boys perched on the upper floor ledges and with
elaborate hand signals passed along orders coming in via phone.
Those hand signals are still used on the floor of the American Stock
Exchange (AMEX) today.

The pageantry and antics of the curbstone brokers congested
the streets and delighted visitors to the financial district in the early
20th century. The brokers wore outstanding clothing in order to be
spotted in the crowd by the clerks in the windows and their clients.
This clothing ran to the spectacular with green derbies, pith
helmets, straw hats, and checkered coats popular.

The heart of the curb exchange was the specialist system,
which allowed for a controlled and efficient market in the less
active and lesser known companies not listed on the New York
Stock Exchange. Today the over-the-counter (actually, over-the-
computer) market has replaced the function of the curb exchanges
of the past by assuming the trading of less popular issues. The
colorful street broker has been replaced by somber pinstripes in

climate-controlled plush surroundings. The specialists, phones, and boys on ledges are superceded by the ubiquitous green computer display.

After McCormick led his brokers indoors in June 1921, trading continued in the street through the summer and fall of 1921. With the onset of winter, police were encouraging the few remaining brokers to "move along." The die had been cast—the old order was gone forever—not with a bang—but with a whimper!

CHAPTER 47

COME TO FLORIDA (1925)

In 1637, the craze was tulips. In 1720, there were stock bubbles. In 1853, it was chicken mania, and in 1925, it was Florida land.

The roaring 20s produced such prosperity that money couldn't be invested quickly enough in conventional outlets. Speculation, as always, was the answer for disposal of excess resources. Florida was the focus of attention, and Miami was the epicenter.

In 1920, the population of Miami was 30,000. At the height of the real estate frenzy in 1925, the resident population was 75,000 with another 75,000 visitors seeking their fortunes. There were some 25,000 real estate agents to service the demand, and the permanent citizens had to put "not for sale" signs on their lawns to stay out of the action. Most conversation was purported to have consisted of the following dialogue:

NATIVE:

"Want to buy a lot?"

VISITOR:

"Sold!"

There were a number of valid reasons for this boom, especially before 1925 and the speculative bubble.

First, there was the climate and its access by the population on the East Coast. Second, the automobile was turning America into a nation of nomads, and the prosperity gave workers the notion that they might have it all. Finally, there was the lure of easy money in outsmarting the other fools. As is the pattern in all speculative bubbles, there is valid reason for the interest at first, but this gives way to insanity at the end.

One of the positive developments resulting from the Florida land boom was construction of the city of Coral Gables on the outskirts of Miami.

Many years before, a retired minister named Merrick had bought cheap land, built a many-gabled house out of coral rock and called it Coral Gables. Now his son added to the estate and began to build a city with Mediterranean architecture. By 1926, he had 2,000 buildings with anchorages, lagoons, and shady streets. His promotion was bold and original: William Jennings Bryan sat on a raft in a lagoon and lectured on the Florida climate. Dancers followed Bryan on the program.

Other developers were draining swamps and piling sand. Lots were sold from the blueprints before there had been any development. Inside lots sold for $8,000 to $20,000 and the waterfront from $15,000 to $25,000. Seashore went for $20,000 to $75,000—not in Miami, but as much as 30 miles away.

The financial instrument used was a binder. This involved a check for 10 percent of the sale price of the lot. When a check was given, the receipt described the lot sold, usually 5,000 square feet of swamp. Title searches and recording of deeds were postponed, and the binder became an instrument of trade. Traffic in binders was immense and profitable.

The summer and fall saw everyone talking about binders and options. The city passed an ordinance forbidding the sale of real estate—or even showing a map—in the streets to prevent traffic congestion. In any traffic tieup, license plates from 15 to 20 states could be seen. People were sleeping in their cars, and food and ice were difficult to find. Everybody was making money.

A lot in the business district of Miami Beach bought for $800 in the early days of the boom sold for $150,000 in 1924. A poor woman who had bought a parcel of land near Miami in 1896 for $25 sold it in 1925 for $150,000. Such tales were legion—many true— but it was all a paper pyramid waiting to be blown away.

By New Year's Day 1926, the market was becoming suspect, and the holders of binders began to worry about the need to make the next payment on their lot. The winter season had not brought the influx of "greater fools" expected by last year's class.

So the bubble burst as binders were defaulted right and left. One man who sold acreage early in 1925 for $12 per acre and cursed himself for stupidity when it resold later for $17, then $30 and finally at $60 per acre was surprised a year later that the entire series of sales was in default, and he was forced to take the land back. There were cases in which land came back burdened with taxes and assessments far in excess of what had been received.

The benediction to the whole process was pronounced by Mother Nature on September 18, 1926, when a hurricane left some 400 dead and 50,000 homeless. This scared tourists away, and the region entered depression well ahead of the rest of the nation. Banks closed and cities defaulted on their bonds. The boom was over—bust began, but Florida was 50 percent richer in population.

CHAPTER 48

BERNIE MAKES THE
DOUBLE-FINESSE (1929)

There is an old bridge maxim that states that one "peek" is worth two finesses. Bernard Baruch was a bridge player who certainly would appreciate that philosophy. In fact, his experience might extend that wisdom by stating that a series of "peeks" can turn you into a legend.

Baruch was an intelligent, handsome, personable, and lucky human who was also an average speculator. This is a minority opinion that will require some explanation.

When Baruch was graduated from City College in New York, he worked at a series of odd jobs until his mother managed an interview with Wall Street broker Arthur Housman. Bernard began in early 1891 as a runner. By 1895, he was a junior analyst, scouting for James R. Keene and trading in 10-share lots for his own account. His good looks and personality made friends all over the district, and he was given "tips" and free rides in various deals. He tapped his close relatives for funds and lost the money. To his father, he proposed a scheme heard directly from a man that intended to build a tram to a hotel on an island in Lake Erie. Baruch's father lost $8,000, but Bernard made it up—and much more later.

What Baruch lacked in skill, he more than made up for in work and personality. He sought out people with money and sold them stocks. By 1897, he had been taken into A. A. Housman and Company as a junior partner and was studying the American Sugar Refining Company as an investment. The U.S. Senate was considering lowering the sugar tariff, but Baruch thought it would not and began buying the stock, starting with his own $300. Margins were at 10 percent, and he took control of $3,000 worth of stock. The price rose from 115 to 156 with Baruch pyramiding his investment, finally selling out for a $60,000 profit. The rise was fueled by heavy buying by Housman and Company. Boldness, luck, and persuasion gave Baruch his first stake.

In 1898, Baruch was commissioned by Thomas Fortune Ryan to negotiate an acquisition of Liggett and Myers Tobacco Company by Union Tobacco Company. Baruch's share of A. A. Housman and Company profits for that year amounted to $167,000, and he now had some big money to work with.

Turning from one vice to another, Baruch started speculating in American Spirits stock on the wrong side of the market. Within weeks of his tobacco success, he was near bankruptcy in whiskey.

In 1899, Bernard caught a break in the stock market with a short position in the Brooklyn Rapid Transit Company and regained his footing in the market. By his own comment: "Wealth began to pour in on me!"

Early in 1901, he got his first clear "peek" at the cards. A broker named Weil casually mentioned that he owned 5,000 shares of Northern Pacific. Baruch ventured the opinion that it was too high at the current price of $100, since it had been 2 ½ in the bankruptcy of 1885 and as low as 19 in 1898. But his modus operandi was to get the best information available, so he called the president of the road, who not only talked to him but also agreed that the price was too high. In fact, he gave Baruch an order to sell 2,500 shares. Weil bowed to insider information and sold his shares at 102. This was two weeks before the corner of NP (Nipper) on May 9, 1901.

Baruch now followed the stock and on May 6, he was on the floor at the opening of the market, buying NP on the London market and selling short in New York—a little arbitrage, with a bearish bias. Beside him was Talbot Taylor, a member of the exchange and son-in-law of James R. Keene. Noting Baruch's interest, Taylor confided that Keene was acting as agent for J. P. Morgan and that a fight for control of Northern Pacific was under way. He advised Baruch to not get caught short of the stock.

Having been given such a good look at the cards, Baruch certainly knew how to play them. First, he bought NP in the London market and then he took a put position in several major

New York Exchange stocks, reasoning they would be dumped to raise money for NP.

On Thursday, May 9, Northern Pacific traded shares as high as $1,000, while the remainder of the market collapsed. U.S. Steel dropped from 47 to 24 and was typical of the list. Baruch cleaned up his position and later stated that the day had been the best of his career. After the smoke cleared, Baruch had some $3 million to work with and a much more conservative attitude from that time forward.

After World War I, Baruch was worth some $16 million (much of it in Liberty Bonds), and he resumed activity in the great bull market of the roaring 20s. But he diversified and played both sides of the market (hedged), while never letting his margin position exceed 20 percent of market value of his portfolio. Before the 1929 crash, he was worth some $25 million and later put the capstone on his legend by claiming to have gotten out before the crash.

There are two versions of the story: Late in August 1929, Baruch was in Scotland, walking on the moors with General Pershing when an uncomfortable feeling came over him. He was supposed to have left Scotland immediately, returning to New York to sell his stocks and avoid the crash.

The second version relates that a beggar on the streets of New York, who had benefited from Baruch's small change over the years, offered him a "tip" on the market. Baruch reasoned that if beggars were touting the market, then it was no place for him.

The truth is that he appears to have lost some $9 million before retreating to cash. At least the inventory of his assets taken in 1931 by his secretary shows his net worth to be some $16 million. After this time, he did very little trading in the markets, content to advise President Roosevelt and other famous people on finance and government.

After being the chairman of the materials committee for the War Industries Board in 1918, Baruch was asked to find a solution to the critical rubber shortage in 1942. Baruch took up residence in Lafayette Park on a bench across from the White House and took the sun and dispensed advice as the "Parkbench Statesman"—thereby embellishing the legend.

CHAPTER 49

OUT OF THE ASHES (1929)

In April 1929, a taxicab drew up to the main entrance to the White House at 9:30 P.M., and a little gray-haired man stepped out. The visitor was told that President Hoover was dining and could not be disturbed. The man replied that he would wait and was soon ushered in to see the president.

This late-night rider warned Hoover that the worst panic in the country's history was rapidly developing. He suggested that the Federal Reserve Board reverse its newly adopted policy of curtailing brokerage loans and security credit. This Wall Street prophet of doom was Billy Durant.

In Egyptian mythology, the phoenix is an ancient bird that lives for 500 years, consumes itself in fire, and then rises renewed and stronger from the ashes. Many investors achieve a similar result, with major failure being their baptism of fire. Billy Durant was such an investor.

William Crapo Durant was the grandson of the Civil War governor of Michigan and was selling cigars in 1886 when he borrowed $2,000 and bought into a carriage factory. Within four years, he had turned it into one of the world's largest, producing 150,000 carriages per year. Around 1890, he met David Buick who was experimenting with a piston engine. Durant bought the Flint Wagonworks, moved Buick in, and renamed it Buick Motor Company. Then they snapped up Cadillac, Oakland, and Olds automobile companies and incorporated the combination as General Motors.

In 1909, he tried to buy Ford, but the bankers weren't convinced the automobile was here to stay. Tight money conditions in 1910 saw the banks taking control of GM, ousting Durant.

A year after leaving GM, he organized Chevrolet, made a

million in profits the first year, and began acquiring GM stock. Eventually he offered five shares of Chevrolet for each share of GM and in September 1915 announced control of General Motors.

In 1920, with GM expanding, the country in recession, and GM stock falling in price, Durant tried to hold the market up by himself and saw his personal fortune go from $100 million to over $20 million in debt. To save GM, the other shareholders voted him out, and he resigned November 30, 1920. When he cleaned up his obligations, he was 60, and heavily in debt. But his philosophy was intact: "Money, what is money? It is only loaned to a man, he comes into the world with nothing and he leaves with nothing."

Armed with nothing, he turned his talents to Wall Street and formed a consortium that orchestrated the great bull market of 1924–29. Included in his stable were the seven Fisher brothers and their $200 million, just received from selling Fisher Body Co. to General Motors; Arthur Cutten, who had cornered wheat in Chicago for $10 million in profits; and Jesse Livermore, who had cut his teeth in the bucket shops of Boston and was always ready to back his technical skills with the millions he had accumulated.

Members of Durant's consortium first got interested in International Nickel and bought enough shares to drive the stock up 60 points, attracting shorts all the way. This added millions to their kitty.

Then they tried Baldwin Locomotive. The Fishers sent their engineers out to look at the company and decided it was a jewel. Their buying sent the stock from 94 to 233.

But this was just practice compared to their technical corner in RCA. For this maneuver, the group added Mike Meehan, a ticket broker turned stock broker. who specialized in RCA.

Radio was a magic name to Americans then. It was music out of the air and Amos and Andy. It was the highest of high fliers and fully priced at $40.

The consortium counted the shares in the floating supply and went after the stock. The bears could smell the honey, and soon shares were being exchanged at the rate of 500,000 per day, even though the supply outside of RCA and GE was only 400,000.

In March 1928, a four-day technical corner existed with Meehan frantically trading the stock on the floor of the New York Exchange. His clothes were torn, and his face battered, but the trap finally was broken.

The stock continued to rise. It went to 570 early in 1929, before Durant made his visit to Hoover. Soon after, it was $300 cheaper.

Managing this multitalented consortium, Durant worked with 15 brokers and a billion dollars, creating a huge public following that helped push the stocks to extremes. But by April 1929, the Federal Reserve was tightening credit when Durant made his secret visit to warn President Hoover of a potential market crash. Unable to affect credit policy, Durant began to quietly withdraw $4 billion from the market and was out completely by summer.

After the market hit bottom in late 1929, Durant reentered the market, fully on margin, and was sold out in 1930. He invested what was left of his capital in Durant Motors, but in the depth of the Depression, the firm failed, and at the age of 75, he was in the ashes again to stay.

Early in 1936, Billy Durant was seen washing dishes in a New Jersey lunchroom. He owned the restaurant, but by the time of his death at 86 in 1947, he was completely without resources. He probably subscribed to the philosophy of the French author Rabelais. "I owe much. I have nothing. I give the rest to the poor!"

CHAPTER 50

CRASH (1929)

News item of October 30, 1929:

"There is nothing in the business situation to warrant the destruction of values that has taken place in the past week, and my son and I have for some days past been purchasing sound common stocks"

John D. Rockefeller, Sr.

News item of October 31, 1929:

"Sure he's buying. Who else has any money left?

Eddie Cantor

Money panics are a fact of capitalistic societies. The boom/bust cycle has gone on—and will continue to occur—as long as there are free markets and variation in supply and demand. War and peace affect the cycle dramatically as do political events and government. The United States was formed during depression conditions with little prosperity before the opening of industrial markets by the construction of canals and railroads.

The first major money panic and depression occurred in 1837 under Jackson's hard money policies. The stock market lost some 75 percent of value in a depression that lasted well past 1840. Twenty years later (1857) bank closures dropped the market 40 percent in less than a year. In 1907, a similar result came from rising interest rates, and unemployment followed.

1929 was not that much different from 1857 or 1907 until the aftermath. The initial panic in 1929 carried the market some 50 percent lower and back to preboom levels. The slow grinding

FIGURE 50–1
Looking East on Wall Street during Panic of 1907

Courtesy of Brown Brothers Stock Photos

Stock markets crashed in October, and bank failures in November filled the street with depositors trying to withdraw their money.

misery of the longest depression in the nation's history worked the market 90 percent below its 1929 highs by 1932. When recovery finally got under way in 1937, another recession corrected the market 50 percent. It took World War II to restore financial stability. In 1973–74, recession and political instability dropped the market 50 percent once again.

There have also been money panics without the attendant economic contraction. In 1962, the market lost 30 percent in three months. In 1987, with the help of computers, it occurred in one day. Computers do everything faster—including making errors and trading stocks.

But 1929 was different in the level of pain produced and the dramatic contrast with the good times that preceded it. John J. Raskob's comment that "Everybody ought to be rich" was believable right up until the end.

There were those who profited by the crash: Albert Wiggin, chairman of the Chase National Bank, was a member of the bankers pool organized by the house of Morgan. This consortium had sent Richard Whitney, president of the New York Stock Exchange, onto the floor on black Thursday (October 24) to loudly bid for stocks, above the market, in a futile effort to stem the panic.

But while Wiggin was publicly supporting the market, he was quietly selling short the stock of his own bank. By December, he had sold 42,000 shares, eventually covering for a $4 million profit. Five thousand of these shares had been sold to the consortium that was trying to shore up the market. When it was time to cover, he borrowed from his bank to buy the stock. He paid not a penny in taxes, as he sold through one corporation and bought back through a second—a page right out of Daniel Drew's standard operating manual.

There were those that observed: Winston Churchill had just been voted out as chancellor of the exchequer and was on an extended tour of America. Churchill's mother had been Brooklyn-born as the daughter of Leonard Jerome, successful broker and partner of William Travers in the postbellum period.

Churchill had been speculating in the American markets, buying Simmons because he liked the slogan "You can't go wrong on a Simmons Mattress." Bernard Baruch took his private railroad car out to Chicago to meet Churchill and accompanied him into New York. Churchill dined at Baruch's home on the evening preceding the panic of October 24, 1929, and whatever advice he received, we only know that he stayed with his investments.

On the day Whitney was jawboning on the floor, Churchill was in the gallery of the New York Stock Exchange—a day that 13 million shares changed hands and the ticker ran four hours behind at the market close. His observations are interesting:

> I happened to be walking down Wall Street at the worst moment of the panic, and a perfect stranger who recognised me invited me to enter the gallery of the Stock Exchange. I expected to see pandemonium; but the spectacle that met my eyes was one of surprising calm and orderliness. There are only 1,200 members of the New York

Stock Exchange, each of whom has paid over 100,000 pounds for his ticket. These gentlemen are precluded by the strongest rules from running or raising their voices unduly. So there they were, walking to and fro like a slow-motion picture of a disturbed ant heap, offering each other enormous blocks of securities at a third of their old prices and half their present value, and for many minutes together finding no one strong enough to pick up the sure fortunes they were compelled to offer.[1]

Whatever his emotions and his personal losses, Churchill never commented. It was just one more phase of his training for the difficulties and greatness that were to come.

Two years after the crash, Churchill had returned to New York on a lecture tour and on December 13 was on his way by taxi to Bernard Baruch's home on Fifth Avenue. Neither Churchill nor the cabbie could find the address. Churchill asked to be let out on the Central Park side of the avenue. Intending to cross the street and accustomed to the English system, he looked right and stepped into the path of a car on his left. His first dinner at Baruch's preceded losing his fortune. The second almost took his life. Dinner with Bernard Baruch was becoming hazardous.

Others who sidestepped the crash included Joseph P. Kennedy, the father of a president-to-be. Kennedy had started as a bank examiner, eventually taking over his father's bank. After the First World War, he managed the brokerage firm of Hayden Stone and began operations of his own in the Street. From a major success with Yellow Cab Company, he moved to show business, forming a syndicate that breathed life into a number of film companies, and by 1929, he was well-established and looking for somewhere to invest his $5 million.

When Joe Kennedy returned to Wall Street from Hollywood, he was assailed from all sides by the optimism of the Street. He stopped in at the bootblack's at number 60 Wall Street and shoeblack Pat Bologna offered Kennedy a tip. "Buy oils and rails. They're gonna hit the sky. Had a guy here today with inside knowledge." That night Kennedy told his wife that a market that

---

[1] Winston Churchill's unpublished "American Impressions," Churchill papers, vol. 8, p. 592.

everyone could play and a shoeshine boy could predict was no market for him. His money went into Depression-era real estate.

There were those that played: Pat Bologna was a 19-year-old shoeshine operator who served the big names of Wall Street. He accepted and gave opinion to everyone from Morgan partners to Billy Durant. More and more people came to his stand to trade money tips for stock tips. And he speculated on margin with his nickel and dime tips.

By October 1929, Bologna had a portfolio with a market value of some $5,000, mostly in customer Charles Mitchell's National City Bank common stock. On October 29, at the peak of the panic, Pat Bologna was faced with a margin call and was forced to sell his National City stock. His $5,000 was now $1,700. Fifty years later, Pat Bologna was still a shoeblack, still working in Wall Street.

Among those blamed for the crash were Jesse Livermore and Arthur Cutten. Both were big operators and credited with more success on the downside than they ever really had. Livermore lost his fortune in the early 30s, and never recovered, finally ending his life in the restroom of the Sherry-Netherland Hotel with a single shot to the head. Cutten, in his own story, never claimed to see the crash coming—in fact, he was bullish till the end and essentially retired after 1929 as a major market player.

Had the crash ended with 1929, it would have gone into the history books as just another money panic, similar to those before and since. It was the devastating depression that followed that made 1929 stand out in the annals of financial misery. Whether the crash caused the depression, or vice versa, will probably be debated forever. Certainly the lessons learned from the experience should be heeded in financial traumas of the future.

CHAPTER 51

SYSTEMATIC—THE
TEMPLETON WAY (1939)

The single word that best describes the great investor John Templeton is *systematic*. He not only uses computers to find his investment opportunities, but he also emulates the computer in routinely inspecting all possibilities, fully diversifying his portfolios to include investments from all over the world. The global emphasis reduces market risk factors unique to a single country—notably the United States.

The Templeton Growth Fund began in November 1954. One dollar invested at that time would have been worth 100 times that by July 1987. That is an annual compounded rate of over 15 percent, while an average portfolio of American stocks would have yielded less than 11 percent. Templeton's performance included only 8 down years against 25 positive years, with a fractional percentage loss in 1981 being the only down year since 1974. The stress on global investments increased over the years, moderating the risk side of the equation during recent bear markets in the United States.

John Templeton has always been systematic. He never earned a grade less than A through his high school years, being admitted to Yale during the Depression. He was forced to earn his way through college with scholarships, part-time jobs, loans, and—here is that word again—systematic winnings at dormitory gambling sessions. Templeton figures that some 25 percent of his expenses were paid from the proceeds of poker games. To be a great speculator, you must first be a great gambler. John Templeton followed in the image of James R. Keene, John Gates, and H. L. Hunt.

Templeton graduated from Yale with a degree in economics, a

Rhodes scholarship to Oxford, and $300 in cash. The $300 went into the London stock market.

After earning a law degree from Oxford in 1937 and returning to America, Templeton began looking for a job in the investment field. Before his graduation, he had written to 100 firms with good reputations asking for a job. Twelve responded, and three offered him a job. Templeton became a trainee in the newly formed investment counsel division of Fenner and Beane. Fenner and Beane later merged with Merrill Lynch to become Merrill Lynch, Pierce, Fenner and Beane, before Smith was elevated to a principal.

Not long after he started with Fenner and Beane, Templeton was introduced to the National Geophysical Company by an Oxford classmate, and John joined the company as vice president of finance. Now he had a good salary, and he began saving half of it.

America was still suffering from deflation and the Depression. The security markets were worrying about the return of deflationary forces and were underpriced. Templeton had been in Europe and saw the effect on the economy created by gearing up to combat Hitler. When war broke out, Templeton decided it was inflation—not deflation—that would occur, and he had a plan.

Calling the broker that he worked for briefly two years earlier at Fenner and Beane, Templeton gave him an order guaranteed to drive any sane person up the wall. He ordered $100 worth of every stock selling on either the New York or American exchanges at less than $1 per share. Here was the systematic approach again.

After some time, the broker reported back that he had bought $100 worth of all stocks selling on either exchange for less than $1 and *not bankrupt*.

"No, no," said Templeton, "I want them all—every last one, bankrupt or not!" Reluctantly the broker went back to work and filled the complete order. John Templeton's portfolio held 104 companies, 34 of which were operating under bankruptcy laws. Ten thousand dollars worth of junk in 1939, but by the time they were sold—an average of four years later—the portfolio yielded $40,000. Four times your money in four years is over 35 percent per year compounded annually. And it was even better for Templeton because he borrowed the $10,000 initially invested.

Like so many others, he had learned about other people's money.

What is the lesson to be learned here? Certainly the fact that pessimism had undervalued all securities and the war stimulated a return to value. But Templeton now ignores economic conditions and just looks for value. He certainly didn't look at these companies before making a commitment.

He was bold and systematic. He played the statistics with a large enough sample to insure the payoff that comes from the tail of the normal distribution of variation. Two of the stocks yielded over $8,000 between them. Conversely he risked no more than $100 on any one issue. In effect, he made 104 bets on a long odds game where there was a bias in his favor. Luck had nothing to do with it!

Templeton subscribes to the fundamentals or value school of investing. Like Warren Buffett, he was a student of Benjamin Graham, the father of fundamental securities analysis. Graham proposed buying a dollar's worth of assets for 50 cents. If done long enough and systematically, the end result is outstanding records like Buffett and Templeton have.

The way you find half-priced assets is to look for temporary distress. Templeton's junk is an extreme example of the principle, but demonstrates it very well. Graham puts it very succinctly in *The Intelligent Investor*:

> If we can assume that it is the habit of the market to overvalue common stocks which have been showing excellent growth or are glamorous for some other reason, it is logical to expect that it will undervalue—relatively at least—companies that are out of favor because of unsatisfactory developments of a temporary nature. This may be set down as a fundamental law of the stock market, and it suggests an investment approach that should prove most conservative and promising.

Templeton adds the benediction:

> It takes patience, discipline and courage to follow the "contrarian" route to investment success: to buy when others are despondently selling, to sell when others are avidly buying. However, based on a half century of experience, I can attest to the rewards at the end of the journey.

PART 6

THE COMPUTER AGE
(1949–   )

CHAPTER 52

THE INTELLIGENT INVESTOR
(1949)

The greatest investor the world has ever known is alive and in his prime today. His net worth is now approaching $2 billion, and if he continues his past rate of return, he will reach $4 *trillion* before he reaches the age of 90. This poses an interesting question. Will he hold all of the national debt, which could be in the same neighborhood, and more important, will he forgive it?

This super investor has no staff of analysts, no ticker service, no computer—not even a calculator or an abacus (he jokes!) Even worse, he doesn't go near Wall Street. He has an office in Omaha, Nebraska, for heaven's sakes! Still don't know who he is? Don't be ashamed, many of the folks in Omaha don't know either.

This investor is Warren Buffett, chairman of Berkshire Hathaway Inc., a conglomerate composed of a variety of smaller businesses and large shareholdings in some major concerns. Buffett owns some 45 percent of the Berkshire Hathaway shares.

Berkshire and Hathaway were textile manufacturers in 19th century New England that merged in 1955. Berkshire's origins go back to 1806, and Hathaway was founded in 1888, with Hetty Green as one of the original shareholders, owning some 6 ¼ percent of the stock.

Buffett started his interest in the stock market while marking prices in his father's brokerage as an 11-year-old in 1941. His first investment was three shares of Cities Service Preferred stock.

Soon after this, his father was elected to Congress and the family moved to the District of Columbia, where Warren ran four paper routes. By the time he finished high school in 1947, he had $9,000 in cash and 40 acres of farmland in Nebraska. The money was used to finance his college education.

After two years at Pennsylvania's Wharton School, Warren graduated from the University of Nebraska in 1950. Benjamin Graham had just published *The Intelligent Investor* in 1949, and upon reading it, Buffett was converted on the spot. He took his MBA at Columbia, studying under Graham.

Graham was a thinker, writer, and teacher, destined to be a stepping-stone for a number of outstanding investors. Buffett is the best, but Templeton is no slouch either.

Graham, like Buffett and Templeton, was inclined toward mathematics, and he approached investing strictly by the numbers. All he wanted was a look at the balance sheet and the issue was clear to him. His simplified, general criteria for investment included the following:

1. A stock should be bought for less than two thirds of its net quick assets.
2. The company should owe less than it is worth (equity).
3. The earnings yield should be twice the prevailing AAA bond yield.
4. The stock should be sold after it has gone up 50 percent or when two years have elapsed, whichever comes first.

Graham was a principal of Graham Newman, which averaged 21 percent for its clients between 1936 and 1956. The four analysts working for Graham in 1956 have each outperformed the Dow Jones industrials in their own investments ever since.

In 1951, Buffett offered to donate his services to the Graham Newman Corporation but was turned down. Returning to his father's brokerage as a stockbroker was not satisfying, and his continuing correspondence with Graham led to a role as analyst with Graham Newman in 1954.

After two years with Graham, Buffett formed a family/friend partnership in 1956 and managed the partner's money to a 2,900 percent increase in 13 years. The fund never had a losing year, even though Buffett's fee was based on exceptional return, a situation that normally invites taking exceptional risk.

In 1969, Buffett had approximately $25 million of his own, which would put him on the first team of investment all-stars, but he was just getting started. He had just bought controlling interest in Berkshire Hathaway to use as an umbrella for future investments.

His approach was simple. Whether he bought an entire business or a minor position in a large corporation, he thought in terms of total asset value and looked for any part that was on sale for half price. Unlike investors of the past, he couldn't manipulate the stock, influence politics, capitalize on insider information, or otherwise take an unfair advantage over the seller. He is a pure investor, finding value the old-fashioned way and boldly taking a position.

Buffett always knows what a company is worth before any offers are made. When he decided to add The Nebraska Furniture Mart to the Berkshire Hathaway holdings, he walked into the store and asked the 90-year-old owner if she would like to sell. It was offered for $60 million, and Buffett accepted with a handshake. Today Mrs. B (Blumkin) at 94 works the 40 acres of furniture as hard for Buffett as she did when she started in 1937 with a $500 loan. Buffett appreciates her as much as she respects him.

Although Buffett and Templeton both adhere to Graham's basic value philosophy, their implementation is different. Templeton uses computers and looks at securities on every major exchange of the world. Buffett sticks with a limited number of industries that he fully understands (communications, insurance, banking, etc.). Templeton diversifies widely, while Buffett concentrates. The Berkshire Hathaway portfolio of investments has shrunk from 18 stocks in 1980 to three large holdings in 1988 (GEICO, The Washington Post, Capital Cities/ABC). Buffett considers traditional diversification to be the Noah's Ark approach to investing—buy two of everything and end up with a zoo instead of a portfolio. The Buffett philosophy is to find something you really like and take a big bite.

The Berkshire Hathaway stock is a small investor's dream come true—a chance to own an investment managed by the greatest investor of all time as carefully as he manages his own money. That's because 45 percent of it is his and all he has invested. No dividends are paid, but that's an advantage now that tax reform has made it so difficult for the investor. Buffett ploughs the profits and dividends of his holdings back into more investments and thereby gives the stock an efficient compounding effect. It's a one decision stock that allows you to defer your capital gains until Congress comes to its senses about investment incentive.

So what's the catch? Price-earnings ratio out of sight? After the market break in 1987, the ratio was less than 13 on 1987 earnings, and the stock sold below book value for several months.

The average investor perceives the price to be too high, since the stock sells in the four digit range (1988). This is the opposite of the feeling that any stock selling for less than $10 must be cheap. The average investor would rather own 100 shares of a $40 stock than 1 share of a $4,000 stock. What they would really rather have is 1,000 shares of a $4 stock.

And besides, who is this guy Buffett? How can I be sure he is real? When Buffett was just getting started and working out of his home, he got interested in his neighbor's kids and asked their father if he had provided for their college. When he received a vague reply, Buffett suggested that $5,000 invested with him might solve the problem. The neighbor considered it, but saw little outward evidence of Buffett's success and passed up the offer. Today he laments that he could *buy* a college had he made that investment.

CHAPTER 53

WALL STREET'S ALCHEMISTS (1953)

Charles Dow was the patriarch of market technicians. He didn't know that because he was dead before his theory was organized and promoted by Samuel A. Nelson, William P. Hamilton, Robert Rhea, and the current proponent, Richard Russell.

Dow wrote a series of short editorials for *The Wall Street Journal* in the two years before his death in 1902. Prior to that, he had joined fellow reporter Edward D. Jones in forming the Dow-Jones Company and publishing *The Wall Street Journal*. Their composite index of 12 leading companies was forerunner of the Dow Jones Industrial Average.

Dow's editorials were on stock market strategy. One of these deals with charting prices in a method now known as point and figure. Others dealt with stop orders and cycles.

But the principles now labeled as Dow Theory related to the psychology of the market being demonstrated in waves. Dow saw three well-defined movements in stock prices. The first was daily variation, which he suggested be disregarded by all but traders paying no commissions. The second was swings of two weeks to a month or more, and the third was the main movement of about four years' duration. His disciples later turned this basic idea into a specific set of trading rules.

The second thrust of technology-oriented investors was to determine short-term trends by reading price action as it appeared on the ticker tape. The person turning this into an art form was Jesse Livermore.

Livermore spent his formative years chalking up prices in a brokerage house by day and completing four years of math at night over a one-year period. On his lunch break, he took $1,000 out of the bucket shops of Boston before he was 15.

To make any money on the low margins of the bucket shop, you had to be very sensitive to price fluctuations and very decisive. Jesse was so good at both that he was forced out of the shops and into Wall Street where he traded chalkboards for ticker tapes and his thousands of dollars for millions.

Known as the Boy Plunger, Livermore operated secretly in a closed office with direct lines to a number of brokerage firms and employed over 20 statisticians to produce data for his computer-like mind. His method of detecting trends is akin to the relative strength approach used by today's technicians.

Also operating in a closed room, and idolizing Livermore, was John Magee. Magee and his partner, Robert D. Edwards, wrote the classic *Technical Analysis of Stock Trends.* Edwards was the brother-in-law of Richard Schabacker, an editor at *Forbes,* who wrote on the technical method in the early 30s. It was his work that provided the basis for Edwards' and Magee's landmark book.

Magee was a senior analyst for Stock Trend Service of Springfield, Massachusetts, in 1953 and decided to start his own service. He rented an office, installed a ticker, and boarded up the windows to eliminate outside distractions. "This room is exactly the same in a blizzard as on a moonlit evening. In here I can't possibly do myself and my clients the disservice of saying 'buy' simply because the sun is out or 'sell" because it's raining."

Magee ignored the fundamentals—going to the extreme of delaying his reading of *The Wall Street Journal* until it was two weeks old.

The next person to pick up the technical banner and run with it was Joe Granville. Joe started on Wall Street in 1957 and wrote another classic book, *A Strategy of Daily Stock Market Timing for Maximum Profit,* three years later. Since then he has written a number of books on the technical method, along with his autobiography and a book on bingo. He also had a brief career in seismology, when he predicted an earthquake that didn't materialize.

Although Joe was never successful in picking individual stocks and finally gave up trying for his own account, he has made a number of excellent calls on general market direction. His predictions are never ambiguous, and his reputation has gone up and down with these confident forecasts. In 1980–81, he was at the peak of popularity, drawing huge crowds for his seminars, and he always responded with a good show.

At the Aztec Inn in Tucson, he painted a long plank the color of swimming pool green and had it installed in the pool at water level. Dressed in white, he crossed the plank to his packed lecture room, creating the illusion of walking on water. "And now you know."

After a minor predictive failure, he came on stage at Caesars in Atlantic City in a coffin shrouded in ticker tape. With martini in hand, he declared: "I'm rising from the dead."

He later told a Vancouver audience that he would never again make a major mistake in the market. His sell signal in early 1981 was on target, but when the market bottomed in 1982, near 750, Granville was calling for a Dow 500. Joe clung to this prediction for four years during the greatest bull market in history and was gone as a major prophet. But he had enjoyed his 15 minutes of fame that Andy Warhol thought we all should have.

Granville's books introduce a number of technical indicators based on market statistics that provide some insight on general direction and interest in stocks. There are no absolute answers, but sensitivity analysis is useful at times.

The entire question of technical analysis is open to debate. There are many adherents, but little demonstration of its success. Dow died shortly after his editorials, but was not inclined to invest on his theories anyway. Livermore shot himself, with his fortune less than intact. Magee spent 15 years charting stocks and never did as well as the market average. Granville never even had modest success in his own investments and quit buying stocks in 1964. Hardly a vote of confidence for the Wizards of Wall Street.

CHAPTER 54

A BELL, A ROSE, AND
TELEPHONE (1957)

Does the spearmint lose its flavor on the bedpost overnight?
If you put it on the left side will you find it on the right?
When you chew it in the morning will it be too hard to bite?
Does the spearmint lose its flavor on the bedpost overnight?

Billy Rose

T is for Telephone. Telephone is Wall Street's label for American Telephone and Telegraph, the billion share company that was the world's largest company before its breakup on January 1, 1984. Its $25 billion market value today is a mere shadow of its size before the divesture, but it is still a dominant public company with worldwide interest. Its origins go back to Alexander Graham Bell and his invention.

Bell was a Scot working with the hearing impaired in Boston and tinkering with electronic devices to aid the deaf. His chief financial sponsor was Gardiner Greene Hubbard, whose deaf daughter was a student of Bell. She later became Bell's wife. Hubbard was a skilled patent lawyer and provided the iron-clad legal protection that withstood challenge for years after Bell's famous discovery.

On March 10, 1876, Watson, Bell's assistant, heard the oft-quoted words: "Mr. Watson, come here, I want you!" However, Bell claimed to have said: "Mr. Watson, come here, I want to see you."

Either way, Watson came and the rest is history as they say. All that remained was to perfect and promote the device and the big opportunity came June 25. This was the day General Custer and his men were dying at Little Bighorn River while Bell was demonstrating his telephone at the Centennial Exposition in Philadelphia. The demonstration was boosted by the emperor of Brazil, who happened to be passing through, and by Lord Kelvin, the famous physicist.

On July 9, 1877, the Bell Telephone Company was formed with 5,000 shares of stock. Bell and his wife, Mabel, held some 1,507 of these shares. Bell was also the company electrician at $3,000 per year.

Boston financiers soon got control of the company, and Bell resigned from the board in 1879 and from his job as electrician a year later. Mabel and Alexander sold enough shares in the next three years to put them in the modest millionaire class, and Bell spent the remainder of his life pursuing a variety of interests.

There were no family fortunes of the Rockefeller, Vanderbilt, or Astor category because the Bells sold their shares much too soon. The one person that should have benefited most from one of the greatest inventions of all time didn't do as well as some early investors—or as well as Billy Rose did 80 years later.

Billy Rose was a teenage shorthand whiz in New York City who went to Washington to work for the War Industries Board for $1,800 per year. This was 1917. When Billy arrived in Washington, he looked around and saw that in any crowd, the head that stood out was Bernard Baruch's. Rose was 5 feet 4 inches, while Baruch was a foot taller.

Billy approached Baruch and inquired as to how he would like a transcript of all his day's conversation. That appealed to Baruch, and he employed Billy for the duration of the war.

While Rose worked for the War Industries Board, one day he was asked to deliver a letter to President Wilson's office. He handed the letter to a secretary and was asked to wait, in case there was a reply. A few minutes later, he was invited in to meet the president. Wilson had heard of Rose's shorthand skill and wanted to talk shop, because he was interested in shorthand himself.

Wilson and Rose exchanged demonstrations, and Billy returned to his office feeling pretty important. When he arrived, he was told that Mr. Baruch wanted to see him. "Pretty good for Delancey Street," thought Rose, with Wilson and Baruch in one hour. The woman in Baruch's office looked up as he bounded in: "The boss wants you to get him a chocolate soda," she said.

By 1919, Billy Rose was working Tin Pan Alley, promoting, negotiating, writing, and editing lyrics, and in general establishing himself in the music business. In 1923, he had his first hit with "Barney Google (with the goo-goo-googolly eyes)." It was a natural move from there to Broadway and then to his Aquacade of 1939 starring Eleanor Holm during the World's Fair.

For 30 years, Baruch served as financial adviser to Rose, and Billy repeated elementary principles that he claimed to have learned from Baruch: Get the facts, investigate, don't take casual advice, watch out for idle tips, study the history of companies.

At the end of 1957, Billy owned about $8 million in stocks. One day he read an ad in the *New York Times* for a class on investment to be given by Paul Sarnoff.

Billy went to the class, but didn't like the attention his celebrity status attracted. He asked for private lessons, and Sarnoff complied. Billy presented his portfolio for analysis, and Sarnoff found it to be diversified ad absurdum. Billy was told he might do better if he put all of his money in either IBM or AT&T. IBM for growth or AT&T for income.

This was a total departure from what he had been taught but followed the advice of Mark Twain, who had earlier suggested, "Put all your eggs in one basket—but watch that basket!"

Rose took Sarnoff's advice, converting his portfolio into Telephone stock, eventually becoming the company's largest shareholder. He also moved lesser amounts to New York Central and Pennsylvania Railroads. Baruch was now out as adviser, and Sarnoff was in for the remainder of Rose's life. Sarnoff went on to make significant contributions to the literature of Wall Street.

By the time of his death in 1966, Billy Rose had some $40 million in his three-stock portfolio. His will was so complicated that he couldn't be buried for a year and a half after his death. His sisters, whom he neglected to make executors, haggled over how much would be spent on a mausoleum. Billy remained above ground in a vault for 18 months. It appeared that he was going to fulfill an earlier prophecy. Billy had once said: "If I can't take it with me, then I won't go!"

CHAPTER 55

SILVER BULLS (1979)

How much money is enough? Rockefeller was asked that question once and his considered answer was: "Just a little bit more."

Bunker and Herbert Hunt subscribe to that theory. Left with trust funds approaching $2 billion each by their father, H. L. Hunt, the brothers are proving that the best way to make a small fortune in commodities is to start with a large one.

H. L. Hunt was a gambling man, and his sons are seeds that fell close to the tree. H. L. gambled money he didn't have on an oil strike that was a bonanza. The brothers have gambled money they inherited on a failed silver corner.

H. L. spent his young adult years as a drifter, moving around the country on odd jobs until his father's death when he was 27. He inherited $5,000, which he used to speculate in cotton farmland, eventually acquiring control of some 15,000 acres. He farmed, sold cotton and cotton futures, and played poker on the side to finance his speculations. The end of World War I reduced cotton demand and reversed his fortunes.

In 1921, oil discoveries at El Dorado, Arkansas, 80 miles west of his farms on the Mississippi, saw him return to his drifting ways, as he took his poker skills to the oil patch.

Soon he was running a gambling establishment, winning and buying oil leases, making and then losing a small fortune.

Broke again, he borrowed $50 and headed for new oil discoveries in east Texas. It was 1930, H. L. was 41 and still looking for the big score.

In Texas, Hunt got close to Columbus Marion Joiner, a man with a lot of oil leases and a bundle of legal problems from overpromotion and sale of shares. When H. L. determined that Joiner was about to strike oil, he offered to extricate him from his

FIGURE 55–1
Silver Prices during 1980 Corner (weekly closing price of silver in dollars per ounce)

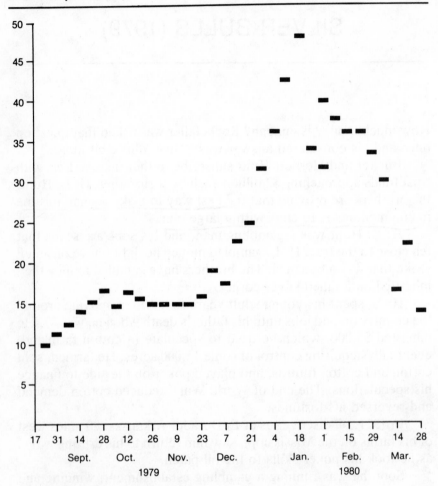

entanglements. Hunt paid Joiner $30,000 in cash, with nine-month notes for $45,000 more and $1,260,000 to be paid out of the wells if they produced. The Joiner leases covered about 550 acres, and Hunt had $109 in the bank. H. L. sold a ⅛ interest in the deal for the $30,000 down payment, the wells came in big, and the Hunt fortune was made.

H. L. Hunt died November 29, 1974, and his boys came into their own. Bunker did well in oil until Colonel Qaddafi took over his Libyan oil field.

Bunker and Herbert became interested in silver in 1974 and ran the price from $3 to $6, attracting silver from hiding, eventually creating a $25 million to $50 million loss for the brothers. This was just a pilot run in preparation for bigger things to come.

In October 1979, the Hunt brothers, aligned with prominent families in Saudi Arabia, made a second assault on the silver market. The price was rising, and equity was being transferred from the bears to the Hunts. Silver was $16, and the squeeze was on.

The silver bears were commercial producers of silver, using the futures market to hedge their production, and a handful of professional bullion dealers, making their living by buying and selling bullion and hedging their inventory with futures. In October 1979, they were very concerned about stopping the bulls.

The traditional way for a short to escape a corner is to: 1) throw himself at the mercy of the bull, 2) get the rules changed, 3) default his contracts. In this case the silver bears chose the second option and went to work on the silver regulators.

The Commodity Futures Exchange Commission was created in 1975 to regulate trading. Its main purpose was to detect and correct market disturbances. In October 1979, the commissioners became concerned about the Hunts and others taking delivery of enormous amounts of silver. This was legal, but rarely done, as the futures market was used for hedging—not as a market for physical metal. The end result of their investigation, however, was to conclude there was no deliberate manipulation of the market. This sentiment was not acceptable to the directors of the COMEX (Commodity Exchange, Inc., in New York City) and the Chicago Board of Trade, as some of them were short of the precious metal.

By January 1, 1980, the Hunts and their allies controlled over 192 million ounces of silver and the price was over $37 per ounce. They also had a nice problem in deciding what to do with the variable margin (equity) that they were collecting. The solution was to buy stock in the brokerage supporting their trade. This firm was Bache, Halsey Stuart Shields. This decision was to be their undoing.

On January 7, 1980, the COMEX board met and adopted Silver Rule 7, limiting an individual to no more than 2,000 contracts, effective February 18. The Hunts and Saudis now transferred to the London Metals Exchange (LME), and silver continued its march toward a peak just under $50 per ounce.

On Monday, January 21, 1980, in the middle of the Iran hostage crisis, which was adding to the demand for precious metals, the COMEX board raised margins, declared an emergency situation and limited trades to liquidation only. The longs were locked in—no one to sell to except the firms that had open short positions.

That was the peak of the market and the beginning of the squeeze on the Hunts. Leverage now worked in reverse. The Hunts couldn't meet the variable margin requirements. Their purchase of more than 5 percent of Bache stock make them insiders, and they could sell only a small percentage on a monthly basis by SEC rules. Moreover, if the stock was suspended from trading (which eventually occurred), shares became worthless as collateral in a margin account.

On March 27, the metal reached a low of $10.80 and the Hunts defaulted on margin calls of $135 million. Within weeks, their losses approximated $1 billion. A consortium of banks, worried about panic, bailed out the brothers by lending $1.1 billion to their Placid Oil Company. Burdened by this debt and subjected to falling oil prices, Placid was placed in bankruptcy in the fall of 1986.

The brothers aren't on welfare yet, as their personal assets of coin collections and Thoroughbreds are protected from Placid creditors. But they're doing a good job of distributing H. L.'s wealth—and in half the time that it took him to accumulate it!

CHAPTER 56

THE DAY THE COMPUTER RAN AWAY (1987)

The cardinal rule of computer design is to never build one on wheels. If this principle is honored and the computer runs amok, you will be able to beat it to the plug and regain control.

The New York Stock Exchange forgot this principle when it designed the Direct Order Transaction System (DOTS), and on October 20, 1987, the computer ran away.

The first computer was designed by Charles Babbage in 1822, without benefit of precision tools or electricity. His crank-powered machine was used to compute insurance actuarial tables. Babbage was known for a number of other inventions, including the postal card and the cowcatcher on trains.

Babbage held the chair of mathematics at Cambridge and established a record by going 22 years without delivering a lecture. His protégé and associate was Ada Augusta, countess of Lovelace, an able mathematician in her own right. Lady Lovelace was the daughter of Lord Byron, the poet, and wrote the first programs for the Babbage machine.

Babbage and Lady Lovelace worked out a system to play the ponies and spent quite a bit of time at the track. At one point, they ran out of cash and had to hock the Lady's jewels to continue play. Unfortunately, the system failed and the jewels were lost.

A century later, the Babbage work was examined by an engineer at MIT and expanded into a theory of representing data by electronic switches. World War II's need for ballistic computations spurred a number of projects to build digital computers.

By 1955, computers were being used by the aerospace industry for engineering and research and for administrative functions such as payroll. The investment industry had not discovered them yet.

By 1970, trading in securities had picked up to the point that brokerage firms and the exchanges couldn't handle the paperwork and the effort to computerize was intensified.

Along with handling transactions, markets were made more efficient with networks of computers sharing order information. The over-the-counter (OTC) market has become the over-the-computer market, with impressive gains in efficiency. Quotation and news items became more readily available to the individual investor, and the computer was widely used to analyze investments for variation and value.

Options products came to the market in volume, starting in 1974, and computers were used to spot arbitrage opportunities. In 1982, the first of the financial indexes was ready for trading, presumably to hedge portfolios, but the low margins attracted the small speculator. This in turn prompted an outcry from each commodity exchange for an index of its own to be used in futures trading. Both indexes and associated futures products—called derivative products—flourished without regard to the state of the securities composing the index.

The index future contract represents obligation to deliver a cash equivalent for a basket or portfolio of stocks in a set number of shares. The Dow Jones Industrial Averages consist of 30 stocks in specific units of each. The index future contract may call for more or less dollar value, depending on the outlook for the market at the end of the contract period. The index can be bought on a cash, or nonfuture, basis, and in a perfect world, this should agree exactly with the index computed from current values of each stock in the portfolio. Doing this computation on a moment-by-moment basis is impossible for a human, but an easy chore for the computer.

So you assign the computer the task of continually comparing the portfolio of real stocks to the stock index, or index future contract, and alerting you when there is a profitable variation in these two numbers.

So far, so good. You're a fund manager and you protect against a major market move by selling an index in proportion to or less than the value of your stocks. If the market goes down, you make back some part of your loss in stocks through the index contract. Insurance! If the market is stable and the numbers get out of whack temporarily, you have enough money and small enough commissions to make a quick profit on the difference. Arbitrage!

A fun game if you have a lot of money and a stable market. No real danger as there are still rational human beings in the process weighing (and sweating) the consequences of their decisions. Free lunch!

However, after cleaning up its act from the 1970 back office debacle, the New York Stock Exchange had shifted its interest from the trail created after a transaction has taken place to accepting the order faster from the member firms. Direct or automatic order entry of transactions has now become available. Just place your orders on your computer and go to lunch. The New York Stock Exchange computer is ready to accept your orders. Computers don't eat lunch.

Now comes October 19, 1987. The market has been going through a period of sustained interest. After reaching a low near 750, the Dow Jones Industrial Averages was at an all time high near 2700 in August. Gurus were calling for 3600 on the index before year-end. The small investor was moving his money from certificates of deposit to stock mutual funds.

Nothing new in this scenario. We've gone through it over and over again. Finally, the bubble bursts. In this case, it was the threat of renewed inflation that brought about a sharp rise in the cost of money. This interest rate spike punctured the overdone air pocket the market rested on and the collapse began. In the past, this might take six months to a year as the bulls and bears skirmish over every point in the Dow.

But this time was different. The humans had gone to lunch—a free one at that, or so they thought—and the computers were in charge. The computers didn't understand greed and fear, only numbers. And the numbers said sell!

So the computers accomplished in one day what could have taken humans months to complete—508 points off the Dow, and the investors thoroughly shaken.

In the past, there was a Morgan who could reason out the consequences in continuation of irrational behavior and provide a compromise. Possibly one of our chess playing computers—now operating on the master level—might be fed memos from the Morgan archives and stand ready to negotiate future computer runaways.

GLOSSARY

A

annuity Distribution of a lump sum and interest over a set schedule of payments

arbitrage Simultaneous buying and selling of equivalent investments in different markets where a temporary price differential exists

B

bear A person who is selling investments—a pessimist

blue chip Top-grade investment—term originated from poker chips

bond A promise to pay a stated rate of interest for a defined period and to return the principal at maturity

bull A person who is buying investments—an optimist

C

call through An auction process where the entire list is read out loud for bids

certificate A piece of paper documenting ownership in a company

commodity Any goods that can be transferred between owners; includes metals, livestock, grains, and financial instruments

common stock Ownership of a company denoted in shares

convertible A bond that has a provision for conversion to common stock

corner A monopoly that allows owner to dictate price to a buyer that needs the commodity to fulfill a contract

D

debenture   A bond or debt

E

earnings yield   Annual earnings per share of a company divided by the market price per share

F

finesse   A subtle move that offsets an opponent's advantage; in the game of bridge, it is playing around the opponents strong cards

fundamentals   Factors such as sales, earnings, and assets

futures   A contract to buy or sell a commodity by some future date at a price set now

G

guilders   The basic unit of money used in the Netherlands—approximately half the value of the dollar

L

long   To own shares; compare to short

M

margin   The use of broker or banker money borrowed to buy securities

N

net quick assets   Readily marketable assets; in accounting terms, the current assets, less the inventory

new issue   First sale of common stock to the public

P

par   Face or original value of the security

pence   English unit of money comparable to our penny

perpetual   A type of bond that is indefinite—no maturity date

point   One unit difference in price; for individual shares in U.S. markets, a point is a dollar

pool   Concerted and simultaneous investment action by two or more

pound   English basic unit of money valued at approximately twice the dollar

prospectus   Essential facts on a company distributed before stock offering

R

rod   A unit of measurement equal to 5 ½ yards

S

short (or short selling)   The act of selling borrowed stock with the intent of buying a replacement at lower prices

spot market   The cash or current market; contrasts with futures

stock-jobber   A person buying and selling stocks for expected profit (speculator)

stock split   Dividing shares into more than one with a proportionate reduction in price

stop order   An offer to buy or sell if price returns to some prior level; a method of protecting against significant loss

syndicate   A pool

U

underwriter   A brokerage firm guaranteeing and handling the sale of a new issue

Z

zero coupon   A bond paying all interest due with the return of principal at maturity

BIBLIOGRAPHY

In preparing this book, I have consulted over 200 references, but the following list was used extensively and should serve as a source for additional reading where interested. Each reference is followed by the chapter number of this book where it was particularly useful.

Allen, Frederick Lewis. *Only Yesterday*. New York: Harper & Row, 1931. (47)

Berryessa, Norman, and Kirzner, Eric. *Global Investing: The Templeton Way*. Homewood, Illinois: Dow Jones-Irwin, 1988. (51)

Brooks, John. *The Seven Fat Years*. New York: Harper & Row, 1954. (53)

———. *The Games Players*. New York: Time Books, 1980. (2)

Clews, Henry. *Fifty Years in Wall Street*. New York: Arno Press, 1973. (26, 27, 31, 32, 34)

Collins, Frederick L. *Money Town*. New York: G. P. Putnam's Sons, 1946. (3, 15, 19, 28)

Conrad, Earl. *Billy Rose: Manhattan Primitive*. Cleveland: World Publishing Company, 1968. (54)

Crane, Burton. *The Sophisticated Investor*. New York: Simon & Schuster, 1964. (33)

Grant, James. *Bernard Baruch*. New York: Simon & Schuster, 1983. (32, 48)

Granville, Joseph. *The Book of Granville*. New York: St. Martin's Press, 1984. (53)

Hadfield, Charles. *World Canals*. New York: Facts on File Publications, 1986. (22)

Hession, Charles H. *John Maynard Keynes*. New York: Macmillan, 1984. (44)

Hill, Frederick T. *The Story of a Street*. Wells, Vt.: Fraser, 1969. (9, 11, 17)

Josephson, Matthew. *The Robber Barons*. New York: Harcourt Brace Jovanovich, 1962. (39, 40)

Klein, Maury. *The Life and Legend of Jay Gould*. Baltimore: Johns Hopkins Press, 1986. (27, 28, 29, 30)

Le Fevre, Edwin. *Reminiscences of a Stock Operator*. Burlington, Vt.: Fraser, 1982. (38)

Lewis, Arthur H. *The Day They Shook the Plum Tree*. New York: Harcourt Brace Javonvich, 1963. (35)

Mackay, Charles. *Extraordinary Popular Delusions and the Madness of Crowds*. New York: Farrar, Straus and Giroux, 1932. (7, 12, 13)

Medbery, James K. *Men and Mysteries of Wall Street*. Wells, Vt.: Fraser, 1968. (29)

Morton, Frederick. *The Rothschilds*. Greenwich, Conn.: Crest Books, 1961. (20)

O'Connor, Richard. *Gould's Millions*. New York: Doubleday, 1962. (29, 30)

Ritchie, Robert C. *Captain Kidd and the War against the Pirates*. Cambridge, Mass.: Harvard University Press, 1986. (11)

Sarnoff, Paul. *Russell Sage: The Money King*. New York: Ivan Obolensky, Inc., 1965. (37)

————. *Silver Bulls*. Westport Conn.: Arlington House, 1980. (55)

Schultz, Harry D., and Coslow, Samson. *A Treasury of Wall Street Wisdom*. Palisades Park, N.J.: Investor's Press, Inc., 1966. (36, 53)

Smith, Page, and Daniel, Charles. *The Chicken Book*. Boston: Little, Brown and Company, 1975. (24)

Sobel, Robert. *The Curbstone Brokers*. New York: Macmillan Company, 1970. (46)

Sobel, Robert. *Inside Wall Street*. New York: W. W. Norton and Company, 1977.

Stedman, Edmund. *The New York Stock Exchange*. New York: New York Stock Exchange, 1905. (22, 25)

Sullivan, George. *By Chance a Winner*. New York: Dodd, Mead and Company, 1972. (4)

Thomas, Dana. *The Plungers and the Peacocks*. New York: G. P. Putnam's Sons, 1967. (34, 49)

Thomas, Gordon, and Morgan-Witts, Max. *The Day the Bubble Burst*. Garden City, N.Y.: Doubleday Publishing, 1979. (45, 50)

Train, John. *Money Masters*. New York: Harper & Row, 1980. (51, 52)

Train, John. *The Midas Touch*. New York: Harper & Row, 1987. (52)

Warshow, Robert I. *The Story of Wall Street*. New York: Greenberg, 1929. (23, 25, 26, 32, 39, 40)

Wendt, L., and Kogan, H. *Bet-a-Million*. Indianapolis: The Bobbs-Merrill Company, 1948. (41)

White, Bouck. *The Book of Daniel Drew*. Secaucus N.J.: The Citadel Press, 1980. (21)

Wyckoff, Richard D. *Wall Street Ventures and Adventures through Forty Years*. Burlington, Vt.: Fraser, 1985. (29, 30)

Many of these books are out of print and can be found only in libraries, old bookstores, or through the reprint services of specialized publishers of investment materials. Two of the latter that I have found especially helpful are:

Fraser Publishing Company
Box 494
Burlington, Vermont 05402

The Investment Centre Bookstore
2124 S. Sepulveda Blvd.
Los Angeles, California 90025

Both firms publish catalogs of their offerings on a regular basis.